To
the best
cook in the
world, & the
Mummy who feeds me!
with love,
Carla.
(Christmas 1991.)

RECIPES FOR A *Perfect* COUNTRY WEEKEND

PHOTOGRAPHY BY LINDA BURGESS

TEXT BY SALLY ANNE SCOTT

First published in 1991 by
Stoddart Publishing Co. Limited
34 Lesmill Road
Toronto, Canada
M3B 2T6

Published in Great Britain by
Conran Octopus Limited
37 Shelton Street
London WC2H 9HN

Canadian Cataloguing in Publication Data
Burgess, Linda
    Recipes For A Perfect Country Weekend

ISBN 0-7737-2523-7

1. Entertaining. 2. Cookery. 3. Country life.
I. Scott, Sally Anne. II. Title
TX731.B87 1991   642′.4   CIP C91-094692-2

All spoon measures given in the recipes are level unless otherwise stated.

The publishers would like to thank Fergus Cochrane Antiques,
570 King's Road, London SW3 2DY and the Gallery of Antique Costume
and Textiles, 2 Church Street, London NW8.

Art Director   Mary Evans
Art Editor   Kit Johnson
Project Editor   Denise Bates
Recipe Editor   Lewis Esson
Production   Jackie Kernaghan
Photographic Stylist   Debbie Patterson
Home Economist (photography)   Jane Suthering
Home Economist (testing)   Valerie Barrett

Typeset by Hunters Armley Ltd.
Printed and bound in Hong Kong by Wing King Tong Co. Ltd.

Contents

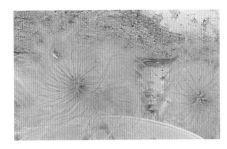

Foreword

I have to be perfectly honest and say that the original inspiration for this book was born one gloomy day in my kitchen in London. Being a city person, I often fantasized about the delights of those long, comforting country weekends, spent being totally spoilt by friends. On that particular day I imagined all the ingredients which it would take to make my weekend in the country a complete treat. Tantalizing images of cool bluebell woods filled my mind's eye; this led me on to the bed I would sleep in – a four-poster with soft, sweet-smelling linen; while from the window there would be the view of a garden spread out like a Persian rug, with a rich profusion of roses.

As I dreamed on, the aromas of the food I would like to eat during my weekend wafted into my senses, tempting me even further. I felt ready for every meal, experiencing that hunger which only exists away from home, that has been sharpened by brisk country walks, sharp fresh air and eager anticipation. I was impatient for loving meals of hearty soups, squeaky-fresh vegetables, golden roasts, comforting home-made breads and lots of fresh herbs and salads with that 'just pulled from the earth' taste. And this food was enjoyed in friendly rooms filled with flowers and glowing fires. Finally, stretched out in front of a log fire, the warmth flowed over me – all worries faded and I knew I was in the heart of the country, surrounded by friends.

Now, with the project completed, we have created this dream. The photography of the book was a great joy, the friends warm and the food delightful. I hope we have extended to everyone an invitation to a country weekend.

LINDA BURGESS

SHADES OF GREY

The Weekend

Country weekends initially became a necessary part of my life to counteract the stresses and strains of a hectic city existence. Fifteen years ago we bought a beautiful but derelict Georgian farmhouse in Somerset. Gradually, as the house was renovated, friends began to take advantage of the very relaxing and unpressurized atmosphere and the house acquired a name that has stuck when, twelve years ago, we were visited by two designer friends, who staggered in bearing a lovely lamp for the porch with the inscription 'Hornblotton Hilton'. The weekends that followed over the years, during which this became our permanent home, evolved quite simply through getting to know the locals, sampling their produce and learning the history of our sleepy Somerset hamlet and its environs.

Country walking is now a part of my life from which I gain enormous pleasure. Nature's glorious free booty, which should never be taken for granted, allows me to pick posies of wild flowers to put beside a guest bed, pluck hedgerow fruits to make into interesting preserves for tea, or gather mushrooms on a misty morning to serve minutes later for a hearty breakfast.

As a working lady and subsequently a working mum, I have always put organization and the preparation of the food in advance high on my list of priorities. Careful balancing of meals, too, has always been a firm objective. I interweave masses of fresh herbs in a meal high in cholesterol, for example, or use sea vegetables and organically grown produce for necessary minerals. Variety in cooking styles also aids the busy cook. Steaming, stir-frying, baking and even barbecueing all produce a wide selection of different tastes and textures. The love and patience that go into food preparation are reflected in its taste and presentation. Conversely, grumpy hostesses prepare grumpy food!

Imagine my delight on being asked to use my beloved home and my lifestyle for this book. I found that the text and the recipes flowed easily and on meeting Linda Burgess I felt that her affinity with the country, her mental attitude and her stunning photography meant for me a joyous meeting of souls. The experience of writing this book has been one of my most pleasurable to date.

BOOTS SCOTT

CAMELLIAS (*previous page*)

It was Bacon who said that 'Proverbs are the philosophy of the common man' (John Gerard's *Herbal*, 1597). Proverbs grow from the continuity of things, indicating a trend or a cause and effect, and to most country folk cloud formation, wind direction, animal and insect behaviour, the elements, the seasons and all that they hold are forces which help direct their daily lives. There can often be a heavy penalty to pay when Mother Nature's potent signs are ignored – crop failure, drought and disease all conspire against those who mistrust the signals that she puts out for us to see. Rooks nesting high herald a good dry summer, free from high winds. Swallows returning early from their warm winter refuges invariably means temperate weather will follow. 'Oak before ash, in for a splash – ash before oak, in for a soak.' 'Holly berries before the end of September – a winter to remember.' Almost without exception these observations which have become country lore still hold good. There is much to see, much to learn in the country, the place where real life stands naked and raw for everyone to benefit from, provided they see with their eyes and hear with their ears and smell with their noses. This is not quite as simple as it sounds, when one realizes the abundance of seeing, hearing, smelling and learning to be done. Any time spent in the country plays a valuable part in that learning process, and a weekend, although short, can be utilized to great effect. The dawn chorus, farmyards, rivers and streams, meadows and woodlands all hold wonderful opportunities to excite the mind and enchant children in particular with everlasting memories. The sheer beauty of a landscape or the peace and tranquillity of a spot untarnished by the two-legged species can be enough to soothe many visitors.

INVITATION TO A WALK
A well-trodden pathway holds out an irresistible invitation to long country rambles.

WELCOMING TOUCHES & GIFTS

Small things from the heart of the host give enormous pleasure. Preparing small gifts can for the most part be incorporated into the daily domestic routine. And they are often free, with many ingredients coming from the hedgerows, gardens and woods. It is my experience that simplicity wins hands down in any competition. The small posy of wild or domestic flowers, rather than an elaborate floral display, or a little basket of seasonal fruit in the bedroom, along with a glass with slices of fresh lemon and lime and a bottle of mineral water, make a comforting impression on arrival. Most people enjoy being spoilt and this can easily be done without too much effort. When washing the sheets, for example, put lavender water or rose water into the rinse. Herb pillows take no time to make and are conducive to relaxing sleep. In high summer, when the herbs are in full flower and the weather is hot and dry, encourage your guests to pick their own herbs and make these little pillows to take back with them.

Herb Pillows

Pretty fabric (preferably linen or cotton), measuring about 25 x 12·5 cm/10 x 5 in

about 2 heaped tbsp dried herbs (lavender, thyme, rosemary or a mixture)

rubber band

ribbon

essential oils

Fold the fabric across in half to make a square and sew up the sides, leaving the top open. Fill the pillow with dried herbs of your choice. Secure the top tightly with a rubber band, then cover this with a pretty ribbon tied in a bow. To give the pillows even more aroma, add a few drops of essential oils with the herbs.

Children in particular love little projects that remind them of the places that they have visited. Making pot pourri with fresh petals and herbs is also a delightful activity.

Pot Pourri

Always pick fresh petals or herbs for pot pourri mid-morning on a dry sunny day, when the flowers are completely open.

fresh petals or herbs

muslin or thin linen

ground orris root

good quality talcum powder or essential oils

Remove any green stalk and the white part of the petal (the heel). Spread the flowers or herbs out on the piece of muslin (or thin linen), making sure that the petals or sprigs do not touch one another, and place out of direct sunlight in an airy room – but not in a draught. If possible, suspend the muslin between the backs of 2 chairs, say, to allow a good circulation of air.

Several days later, when the petals or sprigs are crisp to the touch, store in sealed glass jars until ready for use. When making up a bowl of pot pourri, sprinkle in some ground orris root, strong good quality talcum powder or drops of essential oils (more expensive) for a longer-lasting perfume. Turn the petals constantly for maximum effect and replenish as required. (It is a good idea to cover bowls of pot pourri at night or when away for long periods to preserve their aroma and keep them free of dust.)

ROSE POT POURRI
Fresh blooms enhance a bowl of pot pourri.

It is possible to recreate the memory of a country show or fête for guests by making special little jars of jam, jelly or preserve when you are making a large batch anyway. A piece of ribbon tied around the jar or a pretty cloth top will always produce a smile. Throughout the seasons, there is an abundance of choice for small gifts. Petal and herb vinegars, herb oils, dried flower posies, home-made chocolates, cordials from the hedgerows and nut wreaths for Christmas decorations are just a few of the possibilities. Creatively designed and packaged, these simple, inexpensive items can be transformed into little treasures.

Petal Vinegars

petals such as rose, violet, nasturtium or elderflower
white wine vinegar or cider vinegar

Remove the white heel and any green stalk from the petals (use scissors to avoid unnecessary bruising – small nail scissors are particularly effective), place the petals in a sterile bottle or jar and pour in the vinegar. Use white wine vinegar for pastel-coloured petals and cider vinegar for more vibrant colours. Leave to steep for 4 weeks, preferably on a sunny window sill.

Using foliage as a garnish for food is something that can be done all year round. Flowers and petals, leaves and even feathers all help to create a visually pleasing effect. Try grape leaves under your cheeses, or horse-chestnut leaves with the conkers still attached to create an autumnal feel to accompany dishes that warm cold hands and toes. Silverweed, an enchanting edible wild leaf with a dark green colour and silver tint, makes a welcome change from parsley. Flower heads floating in a glass bowl or in shallow glass dishes make for interesting discussions, and are easily changed when the flowers start to wilt.

Herb Vinegars

500 ml/16 fl oz vinegar (mild for mild-flavoured herbs, strong for the more pungent)
55 g/2 oz crushed garlic
about 2 tbsp flowering herbs, lightly bruised

Bring the vinegar to just below boiling point. Put the garlic with the herbs in a heatproof sealable container. Pour the vinegar over the garlic and herbs, leave to cool a little and then seal the container while still warm. Leave for 3 weeks, shaking or turning twice weekly. At the end of this time strain to remove the old herbs and add a few sprigs of fresh. Keep in a cool dry place.

It is possible to be really creative with these floral displays and arrangements and to use just about anything that is to hand. Decorations using bits of bark, empty snail shells and dried wild mushrooms (if you can resist the temptation to eat them) are further possibilities. Pumpkins, small marrows and squashes make a glorious table decoration, interspersed with autumn vines, Japonica quince, medlars and rosy red apples. Add green walnuts and hazelnuts or cobs in their husks and you have a wonderfully colourful, original display. Lichen and moss are all fun to collect on a country ramble, and even more fun when used to create a decoration as a semi-permanent reminder of that ramble.

HERB VINEGARS *(above right)*
Vinegars flavoured with fresh herbs have a multitude of uses. As well as in vinaigrettes, you can use them to flavour sauces or add a splash or two when cooking fish.

WEEKEND ACTIVITIES

If possible, have suitable literature, such as the National Trust handbook, available in the house, showing times of opening of local sites. The local paper is a good source of information and sporting events, gymkhanas, festivals, fêtes and bazaars are usually great favourites. Characters abound, dialects astound and there is invariably something to please everyone. Some town folk feel a sense of unease when confronted with the odd silence of the countryside, so the chance to get back into the bustle and noise of what they have left behind – although nicely diluted – makes them feel more at home. Often people will head straight for the home-made produce stalls at these events, endorsing the belief that produce from the home and the countryside still rates high above that available from the supermarket. For

those guests who prefer peace and solitude, a walk to the local church or to a local beauty spot can be on the agenda.

Brass rubbing is a useful idea if your local church has interesting brass, and the vicar or rector is amenable. Often on a hot summer's day it is cooling to spend time in the peace and tranquillity of a stone or brick-built church, doing something that can be kept as a memento. Binoculars that children may use give enormous pleasure and of course a telescope to roam the wondrously bright starry skies would put most people in heaven. Bird-watching and astronomy hobbies may start from these early times spent learning.

Recommend to your guests on acceptance of your invitation that they bring clothing to fit the season, and, indeed, to be prepared for all weathers. It is a rare host who is able to furnish every single guest with full weatherproof gear to fit every shape and size. Lack of this important

equipment can mean not being able to go somewhere or do something in the rain. Walking or visiting places in country rain is not the same as doing it in town, and the refreshing feel of rain on one's skin and hair can have a therapeutic effect. Children, particularly, love to be able to splosh through muddy puddles in fields and get soaked from the black cloud hovering so close they can almost touch it, only to come back to the warmth of an open log fire and feel the tingles as they dry out. Encourage them to enjoy these sensations – they may not have the opportunity to experience them very often.

The natural world has many more delights for children. Let them put dead mini-bugs into matchboxes to take back to show their friends. When woodlice, butterflies, dragonflies, spiders and bees come to the end of their natural life, it is both educational and interesting for a child to be able to look at them close up.

A genuinely exciting little project, easily organized for both children and grown-ups – though not necessarily both at the same time – is to go star-gazing. On a crisp autumn or winter evening when the air is clear and the stars look near, put down some plastic sheeting then wrap up warmly in blankets or even sleeping bags. The magic of lying flat on one's back, looking up into eternity, spotting the Great Bear, the Heavenly Twins and other well-known constellations is a memory from my own childhood that I cherish to this day.

Spotting glow worms is another activity that brings delight to the faces of young and old. Again, warm clothing, a clear night, a good torch and a pair of wellies are standard kit for this adventure. Try to resist the temptation to put the glow worms in a jar – they are rare little creatures and should be left to multiply. Either pre-meal or post-meal exercises like these create a talking point for the evening, and a topic for the children to discuss for years to come.

A SIMPLE WELCOME
Little touches like fresh fruit, flowers or foliage in the bedroom are often all that is needed to make guests feel special.

FEELING AT HOME

No matter how well the guests are known, most people feel a sense of unease if their host or hostess is constantly bustling about. Advance preparation of the weekend menu and activities, and baking done beforehand are ways of making sure that unease is kept to a minimum. You still need a flexible schedule to suit all in the party, however. Guests should not be made to feel that they have to adhere rigidly to your minutely planned timetable.

Often people prefer to feel that they are contributing. Let them lay the table, load the dishwasher, or wash up if they offer. For those hosts who like to do it all themselves, always make sure that your guests are alternatively occupied. A wander around the garden with a pre-meal drink leaves time for you to make the table look lovely; or suggest that they could pick some flowers or light and trim some candles. Deploy those who invade your kitchen, the place guests usually enjoy most. Their taste buds are tickled by the smells pervading the house, and it can be extremely irritating to have to dance round those static bodies draped over dressers, holding up the Aga rail or worst of all (and most popular) blocking the main doorways. Suggesting that your guests vacate the kitchen is often difficult – social chat and a pleasant sense of well-being conspire against easy removal. Organizing little projects or jobs before meals is a useful way to get space to yourself at an important time!

Many old houses in the country have their own, sometimes irritating, idiosyncrasies – those creaking floorboards under the bed, the cistern that sounds like flood gates opening every time it's flushed, the second-to-bottom stair that yells in the night as you try to creep past it. It's fun to have nicely written lists in the bedrooms detailing all the minor horrors that might be encountered if your guests get the munchies in the middle of the night, for instance, or simply cannot get to sleep and want to go for a wander. It's highly embarrassing to be heard creeping down the stairs, or to wake the whole household by flushing a very noisy loo after an early morning visit, and full knowledge of the traps and pitfalls can take the edge off a potentially worrying incident for your guests. After all, a successful weekend in the country is about enjoyment and relaxation, for both hosts and guests, so it's worth spending some time and thought on creating the most conducive atmosphere possible.

Spring

PASTURES NEW

The vernal equinox marks the beginning of spring, a time of blossom
and birdsong, cowslips and crocuses, dandelions and
daffodils. The memory of grey winter months fades quickly as the anticipation
of summer is smelt in the nippy spring air and seen in the lively activity
of small animals and birds, as they prepare for the first nest-building
and mating of the season. On the ground and in the hedgerow there are
frenetic gatherings of all kinds of materials. Moss and straw, sticks and mud,
dead leaves and feathers are all utilized in incredible feats of construction,
be it the ragged crow's nest, the beautiful soft feather bed of the blue tit, or the
mud dome of the swallow. All are created with unending energy and fiddled
and tweaked with until perfection is attained.

NEW BEGINNINGS (*above*)

FLORAL TAPESTRY (*previous page*)

Hibernating animals stir from their warm winter beds, beckoned by the warmth of spring sunshine gently invading the den that has kept them safe throughout the cold preceding months. Instinct and hunger ease them into action, and fields and forests slowly become alive again with sleepy bodies going in search of food.

Snowdrops and violets, primroses and grape hyacinths weave gentle patterns on banks and in woods, their colours such a pleasing sight. Pale green shoots and virgin leaves pop out from their protective covers, changing the land-scape so very gently.

April sees the return of the swallows from Africa, a most cheery sight as they soar and dive, performing quite incredible aerial feats, and frog, newt and toad tadpoles are hatching in the still waters of ponds and ditches. Encourage friends to notice these natural clues of the countryside. Spring-time vegetation is young enough not to obscure records of where animals have been, but remember also, when out walking, the most important rule of the country code – that of shutting all gates behind you. Never drop any litter, which could easily choke animals, and never pick any endangered species of wild flora.

If you get the age-old spring-cleaning desire, clean your hard-working chimney by throwing about 225 g/8 oz of saltpetre on to the hot flames once a week for six weeks. It will loosen all the soot, which then burns away, saving you a call from the chimney sweep. Another spring-cleaning tip is to dip an ordinary feather in turpentine and wipe it around the corners of your rooms to persuade insects, and in particular spiders, to lay their eggs elsewhere.

Suggest to children that they make egg-shell collages, or stick spring flowers on to boiled eggs that can then be varnished. Make natural dyes by boiling vegetable and plant material in water until it is the colour you want. Then strain the liquid and soak the eggs in it. Use onion skins, heather, gorse flowers and straw for yellow, pine cones and elder bark for browny-black, and birch bark for purple.

Dandelions can be gathered to make wine, but leave the elegant, and sadly still rare, cowslip where you find her. Sticky buds find a place in floral displays, and bright green moss and silver-grey lichen are wonderful in table decorations. Enjoy the sunshine yellow of the flowering gorse, side by side with buds of broom and the blossom of the crab apple. Use blackthorn blossom to dress your

mantelpiece, but be careful when picking it and always use secateurs, for the thorns are large and vicious. If you get stabbed, make a paste from a little water mixed with bicarbonate of soda. It should be thick enough to coat your finger and you can then cover it with a piece of cotton. This will draw out the thorn and make its removal much easier. Soak the finger in warm water before extracting the thorn with sterilized tweezers.

Petal ice cubes look delightful in drinks and petal or herb vinegars (see page 14) make wonderful dressings, as well as attractive presents.

Petal Ice Cubes

This novel idea is a simple way of making drinks look very special.

Simply add one petal per ice cube to the mould before freezing. Rose petals are particularly good for this purpose. Other useful spring flowers are borage with its sky-blue petals, comfrey, small pansies, cherry, apple and pear blossom, primroses, and violets.

Collect carragheen from the seashore, rinsing it thoroughly to remove tiny particles of shell, then dry it to use in the coming months for a real taste of the sea. Such sea vegetables, I feel sure, will become an important food source as we get used to their unfamiliar but exciting taste. Purple-red dulse is another sea vegetable, which can also be bought. If you collect it fresh from the seashore, roast it in a moderate oven until it is bone dry and crumbly, then either place it in a bag and crush with a rolling pin, or use a pestle and mortar to reduce it to a fine powder. Store it in a glass – not plastic – screw-top jar and use it as a condiment for soups and salads. Samphire, too, is a delicious sea vegetable which good fishmongers often stock when it is in season (see page 63). Try tender young mallow leaves quickly deep-fried as another unusual vegetable.

If you are lucky enough to have discovered where morel mushrooms grow, collect and dry them to enjoy later, perhaps out of season as a real treat. These truly wonderfully flavoured fungi may be used to great effect both fresh and dried. Growing mainly on sandy soil (mostly above chalk), once you discover a good spot for them guard it with your life. The short growing period (March–April) means that they are usually in short supply. If intending to dry them, do give them a chance to develop to a good size before picking them as they shrink considerably in the process.

Drying Morels

morels
kitchen paper
large-eyed darning needle
coarse thread

Morels are renowned for providing homes for mini-beasts, so shake them well first then slice them in half vertically and wash them very carefully. Place the halves on a piece of paper towel and pat them gently until they are quite dry.

Using a large-eyed darning needle and some coarse thread, string them one behind the other on the thread a few inches apart, piercing them through their fleshiest part, and then hang them in a warm dry place in the kitchen or in the airing cupboard. After about 3 days they should be crisp. Remove them from the thread and place them in dry sterile glass containers and seal. When needed for cooking, simply soak them in water for 40 minutes before use (use the soaking water in stocks and soups).

EARLY MORNING LIGHT
Sunlight highlights the delicacy of parrot tulips.

MENUS *for Spring*

BREAKFAST
Muesli Bread (p. 24)
Chunky Seville Marmalade (p. 24)
Poached Haddock on Muffins
(p. 36 and p. 26)
Devilled Kidneys (p. 41)

LIGHT LUNCH
Jerusalem Artichoke Soup (p. 32)
Paupiettes of Beef (p. 40)
Noodles with Primrose Leaves (p. 33)

LUNCH
Tenerife Potatoes with Herb Sauce (p. 33)
Seafood Soup (p. 36)
Tangerine Ice Cream (p. 31)

TEA
Drop Scones (p. 24)
Quick Orange and Lemon Cake (p. 29)
Chocolate Cake with Fudge Layers (p. 26)

LIGHT SUPPER
Poached Eggs on Sorrel Nests (p. 28)
or
Flower Galettes (p. 28)
Seared Lamb Fillet (p. 40)
Leeks Vinaigrette (p. 34)
Crunchy Cabbage with Cumin (p. 32)

DINNER
Scallops with Lime and Sour Cream Sauce
(p. 39)
Chicken with Coconut and Lemon
(p. 43)
Almond Broccoli (p. 32)
Hedgehog Potatoes (p. 33)
Rhubarb and Maple Syrup Sorbet
(p. 29)
Langues-de-chat (p. 29)

PREPARATION

Muesli Bread

WITH NUTS AND APPLE

Make one 900 g/2 lb loaf
Preparation: 30 mins, 1 hr ahead
Cooking: 45-55 mins, plus cooling

350 g/12 oz 100% stoneground
wholemeal flour
85 g/3 oz porridge oats
1 tbsp sultanas (unsulphured, if possible)
½ tbsp finely chopped nuts
1 tbsp freshly grated apple
30 g/1 oz butter
15 g/½ oz fresh yeast or 8 g/¼ oz active
dried yeast
1 tsp salt
300 ml/½ pt water at blood temperature
1 generous tbsp honey

In a large bowl, mix the flour and the salt with the oats, sultanas, nuts and apple. Rub in the butter, blend it well.

Into a small bowl, put the yeast and mix it well with the slightly warmed honey and then add half the warmed water. Stir gently and leave in a warm part of the kitchen until frothy.

Add this yeast mixture to the flower mixture along with the remaining warm water. Blend until the dough is soft but not sticky.

Place the dough on a cold, floured surface, cover with a dampened linen or cotton cloth and leave the dough to rest for about 8 minutes.

Knead the dough gently and press it into a greased 900 g/2 lb loaf tin. Mark the top with two crosses, indenting to about 1 cm/½ in. Cover with butter papers and leave to rise until it reaches the rim. Preheat the oven to 200C/400F/gas 6.

Bake for about 45-55 minutes. Remove from the heat, turn out and leave to cool on a wire rack.

Drop Scones

Drop scones are delicious spread with corn and barley malt, which is available from most good health food shops. This traditionally prepared food is very nutritious and is the natural sweetener derived from the malting of cereal grains (maize corn or sprouted barley).

Makes 15-18
Preparation: 15 mins
Cooking: 4-6 mins per batch

115 g/4 oz self-raising flour
pinch of salt
1 tbsp caster sugar
1 egg, lightly beaten
150 ml/⅜ pt milk
corn and barley malt, to serve (optional)

Put a griddle or large heavy-based frying pan over a moderate heat and leave to heat up. Meanwhile, sift the flour and the salt into a bowl and stir in the sugar. Make a well in the centre and drop the egg into the well.

Gradually add the milk, working in the flour from the edges with a spoon until a smooth batter is formed. Turn this batter into a large jug.

Turn the heat up under the griddle or pan and grease it with a little butter or margarine. Pour the mixture into the pan in small rounds. Cook as many as can comfortably fit on the griddle or pan.

As soon as the scones bubble and puff on the surface and are golden on the underside (after about 2 or 3 minutes), flip them over with a palette knife to brown them on the other side.

Cook the remaining scones in the same way in subsequent batches as necessary, keeping the cooked scones warm between the folds of a clean cloth. Serve as soon as all are cooked, spread with corn or barley malt, if wished, or with butter, cream and jam, etc.

Chunky Seville Marmalade

I always chop the oranges quite coarsely so that the marmalade has delicious chunks of fruit in it

Makes 4·5 k/10 lb
Preparation: 50 mins
Cooking: about 3 hrs, plus cooling

1·35 k/3 lb Seville oranges
2·7 k/6 lb preserving sugar
juice of 2 lemons

Use unwaxed organic oranges or remove any wax from them by scrubbing in warm soapy water. Rinse them well and dry thoroughly.

Using a potato peeler or a sharp narrow knife, pare off the outer peel

Chunky Seville Marmalade

downwards in thin strips leaving behind any bitter white pith. Scissor these strips of peel into 6 mm/¼ in pieces. Cut the oranges in half and squeeze out the juice, reserving the pips. Cut away all the pith and put this with the pips into a muslin bag (an old cotton pillowcase, cut down, will do) and tie up securely.

Cut the orange flesh into coarse chunks and put them into a preserving pan with the chopped peel and the bag of pips and pith. Add the strained orange and lemon juices. Bring the mixture to the boil over a low heat and simmer,

uncovered, for about 2 hours, or until the peel is soft and the pan contents are reduced by about half.

Remove the muslin bag and add the sugar, stirring constantly until it is all dissolved. Turn up the heat and boil the mixture rapidly for about 45 minutes, until setting point is reached. (Use an all-purpose thermometer to gauge setting point at 110C/220F. Alternatively, drop a teaspoon of the mixture into a cold saucer: once setting point has been reached the skin will wrinkle when prodded with your finger.) Skim

immediately, then leave to cool and settle for about 30 minutes.

Stir mixture, if necessary, to distribute the peel evenly and pour the marmalade into warm dry sterilized jars and cover with discs of greaseproof paper, waxed side down. When cool, seal with metal tops or plastic film secured with rubber bands or string.

Label (including the date of bottling) and store in a cool dry place.

Muffins

Makes 18
Preparation: 15 mins
Cooking: 20 mins

300 ml/½ pt milk
1 tbsp pure honey
1 tbsp black treacle
1 tsp bicarbonate of soda
115 g/4 oz unbleached flour
115 g/4 oz wholemeal flour
225 g/8 oz barley flour
1 tsp baking powder
55 g/2 oz sultanas (optional)
½ tsp salt
115 g/4 oz raw brown sugar
30 g/1 oz butter

Preheat the oven to 200C/400F/gas 6 and grease 18 deep patty tins with a little butter.

Place the milk in a pan, add the honey and black treacle and stir over a gentle heat to dissolve. Then add the bicarbonate of soda and mix well.

Place the flours, baking powder, sultanas (if using), salt and sugar in a large bowl. Then rub in the butter.

Gradually stir the warmed milk mixture into the dough, beating well to incorporate smoothly.

Spoon the mixture into the prepared patty tins and bake for 20 minutes, or until risen and firm.

Remove the cooked muffins from the patty tins and place on a wire rack. Keep warm those to be used immediately under a clean cloth. Once cool, keep the other muffins in an airtight container or freeze them.

Chocolate Cake

WITH FUDGE LAYERS

The generous fudge filling and topping of this cake definitely put it in the special treats category. If you would like more cake in relation to the fudge, make the same quantity of filling but double the cake quantities to make two 20 cm/8 in sponges. They can then be sandwiched together as usual with fudge spread in the middle and on top of the cake.

Serves 8-10
Preparation: 15 mins
Cooking: about 30 mins, plus cooling
and decorating

115 g/4 oz butter, softened
115 g/4 oz caster sugar
2 eggs, lightly beaten
2 tbsp cocoa
115 g/4 oz self-raising flour

for the fudge:
450 g/1 lb caster sugar
300 ml/½ pt water
2 tbsp golden syrup
55 g/2 oz unsalted butter
55 g/2 oz good quality cocoa

Preheat the oven to 180C/350F/gas 4.

Line a 20 cm/8 in sandwich tin with greaseproof paper lightly greased with butter, one piece on the bottom and a rectangle to line the sides coming 1 cm/½ in above the rim.

Combine the butter and the sugar in a bowl and beat until light and fluffy. Incorporate the eggs a little at a time.

Blend the cocoa with enough hot water to make a smooth paste. Allow it to cool, then add this to the mixture a little at a time, alternating with spoonfuls of the flour, and beat gently to make the dough smooth after each addition.

Pour the mixture into the prepared tin and smooth the top with a spatula. Bake on the middle shelf of the oven for about 25-30 minutes, or until the chocolate cake is well risen.

Meanwhile, make the fudge: put all the ingredients in a heavy-bottomed saucepan and cook slowly. Do not allow the mixture to boil until all the sugar has *completely* dissolved.

Bring the mixture to the boil and place a sugar thermometer in the mixture. Continue to boil it gently, until the thermometer registers 114C/238F.

To ensure that the mixture does not stick, draw the thermometer across the top of the fudge and a wooden spoon across the bottom, but do not stir! Remove the fudge from the heat and leave to cool in the pan. Once cool, beat the fudge fiercely with the wooden spoon until smooth.

Turn the cake out on a wire rack and remove the paper. Leave to cool.

When completely cool, cut the cake across in half horizontally and spread with the fudge. Place the top of the cake back on the layer of fudge, then coat the top of the cake with fudge. Decorate the cake as wished.

THE OUTDOOR LIFE
As sunnier days return and new warmth
invigorates the earth, the impulse
to move as many activities as possible outdoors
is strong. An old table set up in the
garden provides the perfect base for baking.

EGGS AND CREAM

Poached Eggs on Sorrel Nests

WITH TARRAGON SAUCE

It is a delight to see the bright green spears of sorrel shooting up in the spring garden. The lemon-like sharpness of sorrel offsets beautifully the richness of the cream in this dish, for a really refreshing taste of spring.

Serves 6
Preparation: about 15 mins
Cooking: 10 mins

675 g/1½ lb sorrel leaves
85 g/3 oz butter
350 ml/12 fl oz double cream
2 tbsp finely chopped tarragon leaves
½ generous tsp Dijon mustard
½ tsp white wine vinegar
4 tomatoes, skinned and deseeded
6 large very fresh eggs
½ tsp malt vinegar
salt and pepper
6 sprigs of tarragon, to garnish

Pick over the sorrel and remove stalks as far as the middle of the leaves. Wash the leaves and then pat them dry.

Place the leaves one on top of another, then roll them all into a cigar shape and cut this across into 1 cm/½ in strips.

Melt 55 g/2 oz butter in a heavy-based frying pan over a moderate heat. Quickly stir the shredded sorrel into the butter and stir constantly until it reduces to a soft creamy consistency.

Add the cream and bring quickly to the boil. Remove from the heat, adjust the seasoning and keep warm.

Melt the remaining butter in the rinsed-out pan over a moderate heat and then add the chopped tarragon. Stir in the mustard and the white wine vinegar followed by the tomatoes and cook until soft. Sieve the mixture and keep warm.

Poach the eggs in a pan of water, to which has been added the malt vinegar, until just cooked and still soft inside.

Place the sorrel in nest shapes on 6 warm plates, then put one poached egg in the middle of each nest and cover with the sauce. Garnish each with a tarragon sprig and serve.

Flower Galettes

These thin pancakes look delightful with their sprinkling of colourful flowers. It is up to you which flower heads or petals you use, but please do not pick rare wild flowers, however lovely they may look.

Nectar is a kind of fruit juice, sold in good health food shops, and is delicious poured over the galettes. Alternatively, serve with fruit jam.

Makes about 15-20
Preparation: 15 mins, 3 hrs ahead
Cooking: 3 mins per galette

200 ml/⅓ pt coconut milk
200 ml/⅓ pt skimmed milk
3 tbsp assorted flower heads or petals
(pansy, calendula, violet, primrose,
dandelion, geranium)

170 g/6 oz unbleached flour (or equal parts unbleached and wholemeal)
1 tsp baking powder
¼ tsp sugar
¼ tsp salt
2 eggs, beaten
corn oil, for frying
apricot or peach nectar, to serve (optional)

Put the milks in a saucepan and add the flowers. Bring to the boil over a low heat and let simmer gently for 7 minutes. Drain the liquid into a jug and reserve the flowers.

Place the flour, baking powder, sugar and salt in a blender or food processor and then, using a slow pulse, gradually add the eggs and then the milk and finally the flowers. Pour the final mixture into a bowl, cover and let stand in the refrigerator for about 3 hours.

Preheat a heavy crêpe pan or a small heavy-bottomed frying pan, add a few drops of oil and tilt to coat thoroughly. Cover the base of the pan with the batter, tilting to coat evenly, and allow to cook thoroughly until golden. Flip over and cook the other side in the same way. Transfer to a warmed serving plate, cover and keep warm in a low oven while cooking the remaining galettes in the same way.

Serve as soon as all the galettes are ready, accompanied by apricot or peach nectar, if wished, or with any good quality fruit jam.

Quick Orange and Lemon Cake

Quick to make and delicious to eat. Forget the taboo of eating cake before it cools and enjoy this while it's still warm.

Serves 6-8
Preparation: 5 mins
Cooking: 40-50 mins

115 g/4 oz butter, softened
1 lemon
1 orange
170 g/6 oz self-raising flour
1 tsp baking powder
170 g/6 oz caster sugar
2 eggs
3 tbsp milk
55 g/2 oz granulated sugar

Preheat the oven to 180C/350F/gas 4 and line the sides and base of a 17·5 cm/7 in cake tin with greaseproof paper, lightly greased with butter.

Either buy organically grown unwaxed fruit or scrub them in warm soapy water, rinse well and pat dry. Grate the zest of the lemon and orange and cut each in half and squeeze the juice from one half of each and combine the juices in a bowl.

Place all the ingredients, except the orange and lemon juice and granulated sugar, in a blender or food processor and mix thoroughly. Pour the mixture into the prepared tin and bake for about 40-50 minutes.

Remove from the oven and leave in the tin. While still hot, sprinkle the top all over with the granulated sugar. Then dribble over the mixture of lemon and orange juice.

Allow the cake to cool a little before serving. It's also good cold, of course.

Rhubarb and Maple Syrup Sorbet

Any syrup can be used here, but once you taste the blending of rhubarb and maple others will not compare.

Serves 6-8
Preparation: 25 mins
Cooking: 25 mins
Freezing: about 5 hrs

115 g/4 oz sugar
450 g/1 lb rhubarb
2 tsp lemon juice
1 tbsp maple syrup
1 elderflower head (if available)
1 egg white

In a heavy-bottomed saucepan, dissolve the sugar in 2 tablespoons of water. Once all the sugar has dissolved, bring the mixture to the boil, then reduce the heat and simmer uncovered for about 6 minutes or until the syrup is thick. Allow to cool to room temperature, then cover and chill in the refrigerator.

Wash and trim the rhubarb and cut it into 2·5 cm/1 in slices. Put this in a pan with the lemon juice and maple syrup (and elderflower head, if available, in a muslin bag), add 2 tablespoons of water and simmer gently until the rhubarb is soft. Allow to cool.

Add the cooled syrup to the rhubarb and combine in a blender until smooth. Pour this mixture into a shallow dish, cover and freeze.

When frozen, return to the blender adding the egg white which has been whisked to stiff peaks and process again until smooth. Return to the dish, cover and freeze once more.

Serve with langues-de-chat.

Langues-de-chat

These biscuits are delicious served with all kinds of ice creams and sorbets.

Makes 24
Preparation: 10 mins
Cooking: about 6-9 mins

75 g/2½ oz butter
8 level tbsp caster sugar
whites of 2 large (60 g/2¼ oz) eggs, lightly beaten
5 tbsp plain flour, sieved

Preheat the oven to 200C/400F/gas 6 and lightly grease a baking tray with a little butter.

Combine the butter and sugar in a blender and process until light and fluffy. Add the egg whites and process until well combined and then stir in the flour using a metal fork.

Put this mixture in a piping bag fitted with a small plain tube. Pipe about six 7·5 cm/3 in long strips on the prepared baking tray, far enough apart to allow for the mixture spreading.

Bake for about 5-8 minutes until golden brown around the edges. Remove from the oven and allow to stand for about 1 minute before lifting off with a palette knife and transferring to a wire rack to cool.

The biscuits will keep in an airtight container for several weeks. They are unsuitable for freezing.

Tangerine Ice Cream LEFT *(p. 31), Rhubarb and Maple Syrup Sorbet with Langues-de-chat* RIGHT *(overleaf)*

Tangerine Ice Cream

Satsumas or clementines can be substituted for the tangerines in this recipe.

Serves 8
Preparation: 20 mins
Cooking: 10 mins
Freezing: about 6 hrs

about 10 unwaxed tangerines
1 tsp powdered gelatine
300 ml/½ pt milk
300 ml/½ pt double cream
225 g/8 oz sugar
2 tbsp lemon juice
¾ level tsp salt

Pare off enough peel (without pith) from the tangerines to make 2 teaspoons of julienne of peel. Blanch the peel in a pan of boiling water for 1 minute. Allow to cool and pat dry. Peel off the rest of the skin along with the pith. Remove any pips and in a food processor mash the flesh of the tangerines lightly to make about 600 ml/1 pt of pulp.

In a heatproof bowl set over boiling water or in a double boiler, dissolve the gelatine in 3 tablespoons of water. Stir the gelatine into the milk and cream, then gently stir in the remaining ingredients including the tangerine peel and pulp.

Pour into a shallow freezer container, cover and freeze for 3 hours, until just softly frozen. Spoon this mixture into an ice-cold bowl and beat hard with a wooden spoon until it is smooth, but still frozen. Return to the freezer, cover and freeze until firm.

Take the ice cream out of the freezer and allow it to stand at room temperature for about 10 minutes before serving.

VEGETABLES AND HERBS

Jerusalem Artichoke Soup

This thick soup could be a meal in itself served with lots of crusty bread. For a thinner consistency, use more wine or stir in some cream towards the end.

Serves 8
Preparation: 15 mins
Cooking: 30-40 mins, plus cooling

675 g/1½ lb Jerusalem artichokes
850 g/1½ pt vegetable stock
55 g/2 oz butter
2 large onions, peeled and sliced
1½ tbsp flour
½ tsp ground nutmeg
¼ tsp ground cinnamon
300 ml/½ pt dry white wine
salt and pepper
juice of 2 limes
chopped parsley, to garnish

Scrub the artichokes thoroughly. Put them in a large pan with the vegetable stock and bring to the boil. Reduce the heat and simmer gently until tender.

Melt the butter in a heavy-bottomed pan over a moderate heat and sauté the onions in it until they are translucent. Add the flour and cook thoroughly, stirring constantly.

Add the nutmeg and cinnamon and then gradually add the stock and the artichokes, stirring all the time until the mixture is well blended and smooth. Remove from the heat and allow to cool.

When cool, adjust the seasoning and purée in a blender, pulsing, until smooth. Return the mixture to a low heat, add the white wine and bring *almost* to the boil. Serve in warmed bowls, sprinkled with the lime juice, lightly stirred and garnished with chopped parsley.

Crunchy Cabbage

WITH CUMIN

Serves 6
Preparation: 5 mins
Cooking: about 5 mins

675 g/1½ lb hard white cabbage
55 g/2 oz butter
1 tsp ground cumin
sea salt and freshly ground black pepper

Finely shred the cabbage, place it in a colander and wash it well. Shake off the surplus water.

Melt the butter in a deep saucepan over a low heat. Add the cumin and cook gently for about 40 seconds.

Add the cabbage, cover the pan and leave for about 2 minutes to settle. Stir, cover again and then shake the cabbage. Reduce the heat and allow the cabbage to continue cooking for a few minutes more in the butter and steam. When the cabbage is just tender but still crunchy, season and then serve it in a warmed serving dish.

Almond Broccoli

Serves 6
Preparation: 8 mins
Cooking: 8 mins

85 g/3 oz flaked almonds
900 g/2 lb broccoli
45 g/1½ oz butter
2 tbsp olive oil
1½ tbsp Japanese rice vinegar
sea salt and freshly ground black pepper

Place the almonds in a heavy-bottomed pan, sprinkle with salt and pepper and dry roast over a moderate heat, moving them constantly to avoid burning. When the almonds are golden brown all over, remove them from the pan.

Wash the broccoli and trim it so that the florets and stalks are all about the same size and shape.

Melt the butter with the olive oil in a pan over a moderate heat and mix in the rice vinegar. Add the broccoli and stir to coat with the mixture.

Increase the heat to high and stir-fry for 2 minutes. Reduce the heat to low, place the lid on the pan and cook gently for about 3 minutes. Shake the pan vigorously from time to time to prevent the broccoli sticking.

Remove the pan from the heat, transfer the broccoli to a warmed serving dish, sprinkle with the almonds and serve.

Noodles

WITH PRIMROSE LEAVES

Please do not pick the increasingly rare wild primrose – primroses are quite easy to grow in the garden. Swiss chard could also be substituted for the primrose leaves in this recipe.

Serves 4
Preparation: about 15 mins,
plus 30 mins resting
Cooking: about 10 mins

6 tbsp finely chopped primrose leaves
200 g/7 oz unbleached flour
1 tsp salt
2 eggs
1½ tsp good quality corn oil
55 g/2 oz butter
10 primrose heads, to garnish
6 dry primrose leaves, to garnish

Steam the primrose leaves over boiling water for about 4 minutes, or until tender. Squeeze dry then chop finely.

Place the flour mixed with half the salt on a cold marble board or work surface. Make a well in the centre and put the eggs and 1 teaspoon of the corn oil in it. Using the fingers, gradually mix in the flour from the edges. When almost completely blended, add the chopped primrose leaves, distributing them evenly throughout the dough.

Knead the dough for 3 minutes then roll the mixture into a ball. Rest for 30 minutes, covered with a damp cloth.

Divide the ball of dough into 4. Roll out one piece very thinly on a floured board. Using a noodle cutter, if you have one, cut the pastry into noodles about 3 mm/⅛ in wide. Otherwise, roll up half the sheet towards the centre like a Swiss roll; then roll up the other half to meet in the middle. With a very sharp knife cut into about 3 mm/⅛ in widths. Make noodles in the same way with the other 3 pieces of dough.

Bring to the boil a large pan of water to which has been added the remaining salt and corn oil (to prevent the noodles sticking). Add the noodles and cook for 3-5 minutes, until tender. Drain and toss with the butter and seasoning to taste. Garnish with the primrose flowers and leaves and eat quickly!

Hedgehog Potatoes

Serves 6 as an accompaniment or starter,
or 3 as a main course
Preparation: 15 mins
Cooking: 55-60 mins

12 medium-sized potatoes
2 tbsp sesame oil
2 tbsp sesame seeds, toasted
sea salt and freshly ground black pepper

Preheat the oven to 180 C/350 F/gas 4.

Wash the potatoes well. Slice the potatoes thinly (about the thickness of a coin), but not allowing each cut to go quite all the way down to the base.

Gently fan the leaves open as much as possible without breaking them and put the potatoes in a roasting pan. Dribble the sesame oil into the cuts and sprinkle with salt and pepper then dust with the sesame seeds.

Bake on the middle shelf of the oven for 45 minutes or until tender, then raise the heat to 200C/400F/gas 6 and cook for a further 10-15 minutes, or until golden brown across the top (the surface should be crackly).

Serve immediately, covered with any seeds and oil from the base of the pan.

Tenerife Potatoes

WITH HERB SAUCE

The herb sauce can be made in advance and refrigerated. It is useful for adding to vinaigrettes and is good on pasta dishes.

Serves 6-8 as an accompaniment
or 4 as a main course
Preparation: 10 mins
Cooking: about 20 mins

1·35 k/3 lb high quality medium-sized
new potatoes
1 tbsp rock salt

for the herb sauce:
large bunch of coriander
8 large garlic cloves, peeled
1½ tbsp white wine vinegar
2 heaped tsp Dijon mustard
300 ml/½ pt green olive oil
(preferably first pressing)
salt and pepper

Wash the potatoes carefully, leaving all the skins on.

Bring a large pan of water to the boil and add the rock salt. Add the potatoes, reduce the heat and simmer until tender.

Remove the potatoes from the pan and cover, letting salt dry on the skins.

Meanwhile, make the sauce: wash the coriander thoroughly and combine it (stalks included) with the garlic, vinegar and mustard in a blender. Pulse to mix well and then gradually add the oil in a thin stream while the machine is running, to produce a sauce with a light, creamy consistency. Season with pepper and, sparingly, with salt (the salt on the potatoes should suffice).

Place a pool of sauce on the centre of each of the plates and then arrange the potatoes around the edge of the sauce.

Leeks Vinaigrette

Serves 6-8

Preparation: 15 mins

*Cooking: 12-20 mins, plus 2 or 3 hrs cooling
and chilling*

*8 medium leeks, trimmed, cleaned and cut
across in half*

450 ml/¾ pt vegetable stock

*150 ml/¼ pt tarragon vinegar or Japanese
rice vinegar*

150 ml/¼ pt olive oil

*½ large green sweet pepper, deseeded and
finely chopped*

*1 small can (85 g/3 oz) of red pimentos,
drained and diced*

1 tsp sugar (optional)

1 tsp Dijon mustard

salt and pepper

shredded lettuce leaves, to serve

Take the root halves of the leeks and cut them in half again lengthwise. Rinse all the leeks again under cold running water.

Bring the vegetable stock to the boil in a pan and drop the leeks into it. Simmer the leeks for 8-15 minutes, until crunchy and just tender. Remove from the stock and drain thoroughly. Leave to cool.

Meanwhile, make the vinaigrette by mixing the vinegar and oil together with the sweet pepper, pimentos, sugar, mustard and salt and pepper to taste.

Once cool, place the leeks in a single layer in a shallow flat-sided serving dish. Mix the vinaigrette well and pour it over the leeks. Cover and chill for several hours, turning the leeks periodically.

To serve: transfer the leeks to a serving plate dressed with lettuce leaves and spoon the vinaigrette over the top.

Leeks Vinaigrette LEFT, *Tenerife Potatoes*
RIGHT *(p. 33)*

FISH AND SHELLFISH

Poached Haddock

WITH CAPERS

Serves 6
Preparation: 5 mins
Cooking: about 10 mins

1 small jar of capers, drained
900 g/2 lb smoked haddock, skinned
300 ml/½ pt milk
30 g/1 oz butter
freshly ground black pepper
12 muffins, halved and buttered, to serve
(see page 26)

Place the haddock in a deep pan and cover with the milk. Put the lid on the pan, bring just to the boil and simmer gently for about 8 minutes, or until the fish is thoroughly cooked (opaque and flakes readily when forked).

Remove the fish from the liquid and flake the flesh into a warm dish, removing any small bones and skin. Add the butter and some freshly ground black pepper. Then add just enough of the cooking liquid to bind the mixture together.

To serve: top the muffins with the fish mixture, then arrange 4 or 5 capers in a tight circle in the middle of each and serve hot.

Kipper Fillets

MARINATED IN LEMON
AND LIME

This dish benefits from long marination – up to 3 days is quite acceptable. It works equally well with herrings and is good served as a starter with granary toast or Scottish oatcakes.

Serves 8
Preparation: 20 mins
Marinating: at least 36 hrs

8 large kipper fillets, skinned and cut into
5 mm/¼ in strips
2 unwaxed lemons
2 unwaxed limes
250 ml/8 fl oz olive oil
75 ml/5 tbsp white wine vinegar
1 tsp Dijon mustard
salt and pepper

Place half the kippers side by side in a large flat dish to cover the bottom. Squeeze the juice of 1 lemon and 1 lime over the fish.

Make another layer of the remaining kipper fillets, then grate the zest of the remaining lemon and lime over this layer. Squeeze over their juices also.

Make the vinaigrette with the oil, vinegar, mustard and salt and pepper to taste. Pour this over the fish, cover and chill for 24 hours.

Remove the cover, toss the fillets to bring those from the bottom to the top and then flatten them down again. Cover and chill for a further 12 hours.

Seafood Soup

This soup is even more delicious made the day before, adding the shellfish just before serving.

Serves 6 as a main course
Preparation: 30 mins, preferably
24 hrs ahead
Cooking: about 45 mins

900 g/2 lb fillets of smoked fish
(cod or haddock)
1·1 1/2 pt milk
55 g/2 oz butter
2 tbsp vegetable oil
2 large onions, coarsely chopped
400 g/14 oz old potatoes, peeled and cut
into chunks
1 tsp ground nutmeg
350 g/12 oz fresh, cooked, peeled prawns,
washed
675 g/1½ lb young mussels, cleaned
and washed
salt and pepper
chopped parsley, to garnish
single cream, to serve (optional)

Clean the fish fillets under running water. Put the milk with 575 ml/1 pt water in a pan and poach the fish gently in this, covered, for 15 minutes. Remove the fish from the milk and allow to cool. When cool enough to handle, flake the flesh carefully, removing any bones. Reserve the cooking liquid.

Melt the butter with the oil in a large saucepan over a moderate heat. Add the onions and sauté until transparent. Add

the potatoes, season well and allow to cook gently for 5 minutes.

Add the reserved cooking liquid and simmer for 15 minutes. Allow to cool a little, then pureé in a blender. Return to the heat and add the flaked fish. Add the nutmeg and adjust the seasoning.

Add the prawns and mussels to the soup 1 or 2 minutes before serving. Allow to heat through but do *not* let the soup boil.

Serve the soup in hot bowls, garnished with chopped parsley and swirls of cream if wished.

SAILING BY
A miniature antique sailing boat evokes thoughts of the sea.

Seafood Soup LEFT, *Scallops with Lime Sauce* RIGHT *(p. 39) (overleaf)*

Scallops

WITH LIME AND SOUR
CREAM SAUCE

Serves 6
Preparation: 15 mins
Cooking: 15 mins

12 large scallops
45 g/1½ oz butter
1 onion, finely chopped
300 ml/½ pt milk
salt and pepper

for the sauce:
yolks of 4 large eggs
45 g/1½ oz butter
4 tsp grated lime zest (about 2 or 3 small
unwaxed limes)
150 ml/¼ pt sour cream
2 tsp lime juice

Clean and trim the scallops by removing the black sac and any remaining muscle. Rinse in cold water and pat dry.

First make the sauce. Mix the egg yolks, butter and half the lime zest in the top of a double boiler and whisk over hot water until the butter has melted.

Gradually whisk in the sour cream until the sauce thickens slightly, then whisk in the lime juice. Season to taste and keep warm.

To cook the scallops, melt the butter in a frying pan over a low heat and cook the onion in it until transparent.

Add the scallops, cover with the milk and simmer gently for about 2-3 minutes, until the scallops are just well poached (firm and opaque). Do not over-cook or they will become rubbery.

Remove from the pan and serve in warmed scrubbed scallop shells or dishes with the lime sauce poured over and garnished with the remaining zest.

MEAT AND POULTRY

Paupiettes of Beef

WITH RED SAUCE

Serves 4-6
Preparation: 30 mins
Cooking: about 70-80 mins

30 g/1 oz butter
1 tbsp olive oil
2 large garlic cloves, peeled and chopped
2 shallots, peeled and chopped
115 g/4 oz rashers of back bacon, rind removed and finely chopped
115 g/4 oz cooked chicken, chopped finely
85 g/3 oz brown breadcrumbs
1½ tbsp chopped fresh parsley
1 tsp fresh or ½ tsp dried marjoram, chopped
1 large egg, lightly beaten
75 ml/5 tbsp cognac
675 g/1½ lb lean beef topside, sliced wafer thin
1 generous tbsp Dijon mustard
salt and pepper
chopped parsley, to garnish
spring onion tips, cut into 2·5 cm/1 in long strips, to garnish

for the sauce:
2 tbsp olive oil
2 garlic cloves, peeled and crushed
8 spring onions, (including green stalks), chopped
2 large red peppers, deseeded and finely chopped
pinch of ground chilli
pinch of cayenne pepper
2 tbsp dry sherry
300 ml/½ pt vegetable stock

Preheat the oven to 160C/325F/gas 3.

Melt the butter with the oil in a frying pan over a moderate heat. Add the garlic and shallot and cook gently until soft.

Meanwhile in a mixing bowl, combine the bacon, chicken, breadcrumbs, parsley, marjoram and salt and pepper. Add the egg and mix well to bind and then add the cognac. Cover.

The slices of beef should measure roughly 7·5 x 7·5 cm/3 x 3 in. If necessary, put them between sheets of greaseproof paper and beat thinner with a rolling pin. Spread each slice with mustard and then season well. Spoon the stuffing equally over each slice. Roll up into little packages, tucking in the ends to contain the stuffing. Tie each paupiette carefully with butcher's string.

Place the paupiettes in the pan with the garlic and shallot and over a moderate to high heat brown them all over. Place in a casserole and cover. Cook in the oven for 50 minutes. Remove the lid, increase the oven temperature to 200C/400F/gas 6 and cook for a further 5 minutes. Turn the paupiettes at least twice during the cooking.

Meanwhile, make the sauce: place the oil in a heavy-bottomed pan over a moderate heat and cook the garlic, spring onions and peppers until soft and tender.

Stir in the chilli, cayenne and salt and cook for a further 1 minute. Add the liquids and bring to the boil, then simmer to reduce the sauce slightly.

Liquidize the mixture then strain it through a fine sieve. Put the sieved sauce into a clean pan and warm through gently. Take the strings off the cooked paupiettes, put them on a warmed serving dish and coat them with the sauce to serve.

Seared Lamb Fillet

WITH LEMON THYME

Serves 6
Preparation: 10 mins
Cooking: about 5 mins

12 sprigs of lemon thyme
1 tbsp olive oil
55 g/2 oz butter
675 g/1½ lb lamb fillet, sliced into 6 mm/¼ in thick discs
1 tbsp lemon pepper
salt and pepper

Put 8 of the thyme sprigs in a heatproof bowl and pour 200 ml/⅓ pt of boiling water over them. Leave the thyme to infuse for a few minutes. Chop the remaining sprigs.

Heat a ridged steak pan over a high heat and put half of the oil and butter on the pan. (Do not allow the fats to burn!) Place the lamb pieces on the pan so that they sear as they touch and leave to cook for about 1 minute. Turn and cook similarly on the other side. (The meat should stay quite pink on the inside.) Transfer the lamb to a warmed serving dish and keep warm.

Add the rest of the oil and butter to the fats already in the pan along with the lemon pepper. Slowly increase the heat and gradually add the thyme infusion, including the leaves.

Allow to bubble, adding salt and pepper to taste, then quickly pour the sauce, including the thyme sprigs, over the meat. Sprinkle the chopped thyme over the top and serve immediately.

CLOTH OF GOLD
Sunny rape flowers swathe the fields as far as the eye can see.

Devilled Kidneys

The perfect hearty breakfast!

Serves 6
Preparation: 15 mins
Cooking: about 15 mins

12 lambs' kidneys
2 tbsp butter
2 tbsp corn oil
1 large onion, peeled and diced
115 g/4 oz flat mushrooms, wiped, trimmed
and chopped
2 tsp Dijon mustard
1 tsp mushroom ketchup
4 tsp Worcestershire sauce
¼ tsp cayenne
sea salt and black pepper

Halve the kidneys, removing any membranes and the white cores. Rinse and then pat dry.

Heat half the butter with the oil in a frying pan over a moderate heat and gently fry the kidney halves for about 4 minutes on each side. Remove the kidneys from the pan, transfer to a flame-proof dish and keep warm.

Place the onion in the pan and cook slowly in the juices until softened and then add the mushrooms. Stir until cooked. Add the remaining butter and allow it to melt, then add the mustard, ketchup and Worcestershire sauce, stirring all the time.

Preheat a hot grill.

Raise the heat slightly under the mushroom mixture, then add the cayenne, mixing it thoroughly. Add enough water to make a sauce. Allow this sauce to bubble for about 30 seconds, then pour it over the kidneys and grill for about 1 minute.

Serve immediately with toast.

Chicken

WITH COCONUT AND LEMON

Serves 6-8
Preparation: 15 mins
Cooking: 15-20 min per 450 g/1 lb plus
about 10 mins

1 fresh chicken, dressed weight about
2·3 k/5 lb
4 unwaxed lemons
1 tin (125 g/4½ oz) of coconut milk
85 g/3 oz butter, softened
salt and pepper

Preheat the oven to 200C/400F/gas 6.

Quarter 3 of the lemons. Rinse out the cavity of the chicken and drain well. Stuff loosely with the lemon quarters and place the bird in the roasting pan.

Using the blunt rounded handle of a spoon, gently pull back the skin over each breast without puncturing it. Spread the thick, paste-like part of the coconut milk evenly over the breasts. Lay the skin back in place.

Spread the butter over the entire breast down to the legs. Season the bird well all over. Fill the cavity with the remaining coconut milk then stuff the end with the whole lemon, skin side out.

Pour 150 ml/¼ pt of water into the pan and roast the bird for 15-20 minutes per 450 g/1 lb, basting from time to time.

20 minutes before the end of cooking time, keeping the bird in the pan, squash the lemons inside the cavity with the back end of a spoon to release the juices. Gently raise the bird and empty most of the cavity juices into the juices in the pan. If the bird is not sufficiently browned, turn the heat up slightly for the final period of cooking.

Take the chicken out of the pan. Remove and discard the lemons from the bird, squashing again to release any juices into the sauce. Carefully empty the cavity juices into the roasting pan. Place the bird on a warmed serving dish.

Place the roasting pan over a high heat and bring the sauce to the boil. Adjust the seasoning and add more butter or water as necessary. Carve the bird and serve the sauce separately.

Chicken with Coconut and Lemon (left)
CLOUDS OF COW PARSLEY (*above*)

Summer

Summer is the season when the living community functions at its fullest:
vegetation supports a huge number and great diversity of animals, birds, and
insects and with summer's fruit and flowers, leaves and roots,
sap and bark there is an abundance of food for the busy raising of the young.
The fields and hedgerows are literally blooming, overflowing with colours and
smells. Take children for rambles through meadows full of clover;
search for ladybirds and spiders and explain how they aid the farmer in
controlling aphids, bugs and beetles that would otherwise chomp their way
through crops at an alarming rate; and revel with them in their childish delight
at the wonders that surround them in this season at every
glance and every step.

RESTING AMONG THE HERBS (*above*)

SUMMER ABUNDANCE (*previous page*)

From June through to September you can go badger-watching (make sure you are always downwind of the set). Although shy, when they are unaware of a human presence these sturdy creatures are boisterous and mischievous in play, and with a long lens it's possible to take magical photographs. In July and August pick reeds and rushes to make rough baskets, by wetting them before plaiting and weaving. Encourage children to learn about bats that fly in the late-evening skies. These fascinating nocturnal mammals do great work in pest control, so if they do make a home on your patch, welcome them to stay. The timbers around their nesting area will be kept completely free of that devastating insect, the boring beetle, which can be so destructive in homes with elderly timbers.

Crystallized Petals and Flowers

Quite a variety of flowers suit this treatment as they keep their colour well: borage, lavender, marigold (calendula, *not* African Tagetes which is poisonous), rose and individual rose petals, violet, primrose and daisy.

If the flowers need only last a few days: whisk an egg white until frothy and sticky but not stiff. Paint the flowers and petals on all sides. Then immediately dust them with caster sugar and allow them to dry at room temperature until crisp. Store in an airtight container.

If the flowers have to last a few weeks: mix together 2 tablespoons of vodka or gin and 1 teaspoon of gum arabic, paint the flowers with this mixture and dust well with sugar as described above. Shake off any surplus caster sugar and leave the flowers to dry until crisp. Store in an airtight container.

Flower and Petal Ice Bowl

Present the ice bowl on a tray or dish deep enough to accommodate extra flower heads that can be scattered over to float as the sculpture unfreezes. This takes about 1-2 hours depending on the room temperature.

Place 4-6 ice cubes into the base of a large freezer-proof bowl, then place a smaller bowl (approximately one third smaller) into the large bowl, weighting it down to hold it in place. Poured iced water into the gap, and arrange flowers and foliage of your choice in the water, with their heads pointing outwards. (You may need to use extra ice cubes to anchor them in place.) Top up with extra iced water, if necessary, to come up to the rim of the bowl, then freeze until completely solid.

Remove from the freezer and leave at room temperature for about half an hour. The inner bowl should then come away quite easily. If it does not, dip the whole thing into warm water and wiggle the inner bowl until it becomes loose and you can remove the ice mould. Replace in the freezer until required.

Blueberries can be dried now and kept for making blueberry vinegar in winter (see page 106). A rewarding project in which children can join is crystallizing flower heads and petals. They look quite beautiful, taste good, and cheer up all sorts of cakes and puddings. Iced petals and flowers are fun to make into a centrepiece.

Picnics can be such fun and, when food is prepared in advance, little trouble to pack. Mousses and terrines, tarts and cold soups make delicious spreads to enjoy while watching cricket or polo, or when fishing or at a gymkhana.

Keep in mind colour and texture, as well as taste, when deciding on the menu and your spread will resemble a feast. In these days of thermal flasks, ice boxes and lightweight picnic equipment, a wonderfully relaxed day in the summer sunshine can be guaranteed.

Go mad with salads while so much is available both from our fertile soil and imported from abroad. Combine tropical fruits with grilled goat's cheese and make warm oil vinaigrettes; watercress, beetroot and clementine marry well in a salad, and for garnishes and dressings you can be generous with fresh herbs, which also aid health in a delicious way.

If guests become weary from all the activity, the change of air, or a simple indulgence in good plain food, give them parsley honey at bed-time and they will quickly be restored. This natural restorative can be made by anyone with an ample supply of parsley from their garden or window box.

Make elderflower champagne (see page 52), in which the scent of the flowers still comes through. Boil camomile flowers in water, then strain and use the liquid to rinse your hair after a shampoo. Its natural dye adds lustre to blonde hair, as do hops, which can be used in the same way for a rinse for brunettes.

Use the extraordinary, bright blue flowers of borage to dress cakes and salads. Wild dogrose petals are particularly good for this purpose, too, as they have dark edges graduating to pale pink centres. Comfrey, quickly blanched, can be applied to bruises and bandaged on overnight. You will be amazed at how quickly the bruising will go down. Pick hedgerow weeds to make lovely floral displays, both large and small. A posy of buttercups and cow parsley can be quite simply exquisite. Mallow and meadowsweet interspersed with any of the fresh mints make a lovely smelling vase to place in guests' bedrooms. Roses, of course, find their way into homes everywhere in this season. Sweet-scented sweetpeas with their vibrant shades create fine splashes of colour, and the wonderfully frail-looking poppy amidst the golden, ripening corn remains an eternal summer sight.

Outdoor theatre and the much-loved barbecue, the seaside and the river bank are places to enjoy during the gentle weather of this season. Sunshine soothes the soul and makes people more sociable, and painting and poetry, weaving and writing can be indulged in while soaking up the atmosphere of the countryside and inhaling fresh air.

Parsley Honey

Parsley is a most valuable and versatile herb and has marvellous healing powers. This honey can simply be eaten to enliven tired minds and bodies, or it may also be used as an alternative to more usual table condiments.

Fills three 450 g/1 lb jars

115 g/4 oz fresh parsley, chopped
900 g/2 lb unbleached granulated sugar

Put the parsley into a pan with 1·1 1/2 pt hot water and leave to infuse for 20 minutes, then bring the water to the boil. The colour should drain from the parsley into the water.

Immediately strain off the liquid and add the sugar. Return the liquid to a moderate heat to dissolve the sugar, stirring constantly, then bring to the boil and continue to boil until the liquid starts to thicken.

Remove from the heat and pour into warm dry sterilized screw-topped glass jars. Seal and label.

PAINTERLY COLOUR
Nature competes with art in this splash of summer red against a richly painted canvas.

THE SEASON'S RICHES *(overleaf)*
The vegetable and fruit gardens overflow with ripe, delicious produce.

MENUS *for Summer*

BREAKFAST
Stuffed Croissants (p. 52 and p. 64)

LIGHT LUNCH
Rich Minted Yoghurt Soup (p. 55)
Mange-Tout Peas with Prawns and Mock Caviar (p. 61)
Gooseberry Fool (p. 68)

LUNCH
Watercress Soup (p. 55)
Garlic and Herb Bread (p. 52)
Buckwheat Pancakes with Smoked Eel and Sour Cream (p. 61)
Rosé and Rose Petal Sorbet (p. 71)

TEA
Scones (p. 53)
Japonica Jam (p. 53)
Melting Moments (p. 54)

LIGHT SUPPER
Chilled Apricot Soup (p. 57)
Pork Fillet with Purple Sage Butter (p. 64)
or
Halibut Steaks with Samphire (p. 63)
Summer Vegetables (p. 59)
Broad Beans with Pine Nuts and Basil Sauce (p. 60)
Marzipan Strawberries (p. 68)

DINNER
Chilled Lebanese Soup (p. 55)
Salmon with Fresh Ginger and Mustard Flower Sauce (p. 64)
or
Brick-Baked Lamb with Lavender and Hay (p. 67)
Herbed New Potatoes (p. 58)
Haricots Verts with Caper Leaf Vinaigrette (p. 58)
Jewel Tart with Marigold Cream (p. 72)

PREPARATION

Elderflower Champagne

Makes about 4·5 l/8 pt
Preparation: 10 mins
Cooking: about 25 mins, 10 days ahead

8 large flowering heads of elder
4·5 l/8 pt of spring water or
filtered tap water
550 g/1¼ lb unbleached granulated sugar
2 unwaxed lemons, sliced and pips removed
2 tbsp white wine vinegar

Shake the elderflower heads well to rid them of any clinging insects. Rinse and pat the flowers dry with paper towels.

In a large pan, bring the water to the boil and remove from the heat once boiling. Immediately dissolve the granulated sugar in the water, stirring constantly. Leave to cool.

When completely cool, add the flower heads, lemon slices and vinegar. Leave for 48 hours.

At the end of this time, strain the liquid carefully through a muslin cloth and then transfer to dry, sterilized, long-necked, clear glass bottles with corks.

As with real champagne, the contents of the bottles can become very lively, so it is recommended that the corks be wired for safety.

The elderflower champagne is ready to drink after 8 days. Serve well chilled as a fizzy, heady and delicious aperitif.

Garlic and Herb Bread

Makes two 900 g/2 lb
(or four 450 g/1 lb) loaves
Preparation: 15 mins plus 30 mins proving
Cooking: 40-50 mins, plus cooling

1·35 k/3 lb pure wholemeal flour
1 tbsp fine sea salt
4 tbsp oregano (chopped fresh, if possible)
4 tsp chopped fresh young rosemary
2 tsp chopped fresh thyme
1½ tsp ground turmeric
24 garlic cloves, peeled and diced
1 large onion, peeled and diced (optional)
700 ml/1¼ pt warm water
30 g/1 oz fresh yeast
1 tbsp raw cane sugar

Put the flour into a large mixing bowl and mix in the salt, herbs and spices and garlic (and onion, if using).

Into 150 ml/¼ pt of the warm water, crumble the yeast along with the sugar. Leave for 10-15 minutes in a warm place until it becomes frothy.

Pour the yeast mixture slowly into the flour mixture and gradually incorporate the remaining warm water. Using the hands, mix the ingredients together thoroughly, then divide the dough into 2 equal balls.

Grease two 23 cm/9 in loaf tins with a little butter or oil. Slightly warm the 2 prepared loaf tins and then place a ball of dough in each. Cover each with a dampened linen or cotton cloth, place in a warm spot and allow to rise just above the rim of the tin.

Preheat the oven to 200C/400F/gas 6. Quickly put them in the oven and bake for about 40 minutes, until the bases sound hollow when tapped.

Loosen the sides of the loaves from the tins, leave to cool a little then turn out on a wire rack to cool completely.

Croissants

Makes 12
Preparation: 2 hrs, plus chilling
Cooking: 20 mins

450 g/1 lb strong plain white flour, sifted
30 g/1 oz vegetable lard, cut into
small pieces
2 tsp salt
30 g/1 oz fresh yeast
300 ml/½ pt warm water
2 eggs
170 g/6 oz butter
½ tsp caster sugar

Place the flour in a large bowl with the lard and rub the lard into the flour with the fingertips until the mixture looks like large breadcrumbs. Add the salt, mix and make a well in the centre.

Cream the yeast in the warm water with a fork until frothy and then add this to the well along with one of the eggs. Using the fingertips again, blend in the flour and then beat the dough until it leaves the sides of the bowl cleanly.

Put the dough on a lightly floured cool surface and knead it for about 10 minutes until smooth.

Soften the butter slightly with a wooden spoon, until it is pliable and creamy but not too soft, then divide it into 3 roughly equal portions.

Roll the dough out into a rectangle about 50 x 20 cm/20 x 8 in, which is about 6 mm/¼ in thick. Trim, if necessary.

Dot one portion of the butter over two-thirds of the length of the dough, also leaving a 1 cm/½ in border around all the edges. Fold the dough in three, bringing up and in the unbuttered one-third first and then folding in the opposite third. Turn the dough a half turn and then seal the edges by pressing them with the rolling pin.

Again pressing with the rolling pin, shape the dough into a long strip and roll into a rectangle as before. Repeat the process of dotting with butter, folding in and turning the dough. Repeat this entire process for a third time. At all times try to keep the corners of the dough square and the edges straight.

Wrap the dough in a dampened linen, cotton or muslin cloth and chill for 45 minutes.

Repeat the rolling and folding process 3 more times (although *not* dotting with butter), turning a half turn each time and allowing the dough to rest and chill wrapped in the cloth for 45 minutes between each process.

After a final chilling, roll the pastry out on a lightly floured surface into a rectangle about 62·5 x 32·5 cm/25 x 13 in. Cover again and leave to rest at room temperature for 10 minutes.

Cut the dough in two and trim into two 30 cm/12 in squares. Cut each of these in half and then cut the halves into 3 triangles with 15 cm/6 in bases.

In a small bowl, place the other egg and beat it lightly, then add the sugar and about 6 drops of water. Mix together well. Using a pastry bush, paint the pastry triangles with the egg wash.

Loosely roll up the triangles from the bottom edge. Leaving the tip on the underside, carefully mould them into crescent shapes.

Place the croissants on a baking tray and glaze them lightly again with the egg wash. Cover with greaseproof paper and leave to prove for about 40 minutes at room temperature.

Preheat the oven to 220C/425F/gas 7.

At the end of the proving time, give the croissants another quick coating of glaze and then place the tray in the middle of the oven and bake for 17-20 minutes, until golden brown.

Ease the cooked croissants from the tray using a palette knife if necessary. Allow them to cool slightly on a wire rack before filling. (see page 64).

Scones

Makes 12
Preparation: 15 mins
Cooking: 10-12 mins

60 g/2¼ oz butter
170 g/6 oz sour cream
(or equal parts sour cream and milk)
1 egg
285 g/10 oz self-raising flour, sifted
pinch of salt
1 egg yolk, beaten (optional)

Preheat the oven to 230C/450F/gas 8 and lightly grease a baking tray with a little butter.

Melt the butter gently in a large pan over a low heat and then add to the sour cream (or cream and milk mixture) along with the egg. Stir in the flour and salt and mix to a smooth dough.

Turn the dough out on a slightly floured surface which is as cold as possible (marble is ideal) and knead lightly for about 2 minutes. Pat the dough flat with the palm of the hand until it is about 2 cm/¾ in thick. Using a 5 cm/2 in scone cutter, cut the dough into rounds. Place on the prepared baking sheet, brush with beaten egg yolk, if wished, and bake the scones for about 10-12 minutes until golden brown.

Japonica Jam

Japonica quinces, slightly larger than crab apples and a pale golden colour, make beautiful jam with a distinctive flavour.

Makes about 2·3 k/4 lb
Preparation: 10 mins
Cooking: 30 mins, plus cooling

1·8 k/4 lb Japonica quinces
granulated sugar
1 heaped tsp ground cloves

Wash the fruit and chop it into rough chunks. Place these in a pan with 7 l/4 pt water. Bring to the boil and then allow to boil gently until the flesh is tender. Allow to cool and then sieve.

Weigh the pulp and water and then add an equal weight of sugar. Return to the pan and bring to the boil again, stirring constantly. Add the cloves and continue to boil.

After about 10 minutes boiling, start doing the setting test (see Chunky Seville Marmalade, page 24).

When it is ready, pour the jam into warmed dry sterilized glass jars and seal immediately with screw-tops or discs of greaseproof paper, cellophane and elastic bands as for Chunky Seville Marmalade.

Melting Moments

WITH CHOCOLATE COATING

You can omit the chocolate if you would just like plain biscuits.

Makes about 40
Preparation: 20 mins
Cooking: 15 mins, plus cooling and decorating

55 g/2 oz icing sugar, sifted
225 g/8 oz butter
55 g/2 oz cornflour
170 g/6 oz flour
30 g/1oz vegetable shortening
2 tsp grated zest from an unwaxed orange
225 g/8 oz dark chocolate (or equal parts dark chocolate and milk)

Preheat the oven to 180C/350F/gas 4 and lightly grease a baking sheet with a little butter.

Cream the icing sugar with the butter in a bowl until the mixture is light and fluffy. Gradually add the cornflour and then the plain flour, mixing thoroughly.

Put the mixture into a piping bag fitted with a large fluted nozzle and pipe small stars of the mixture on the prepared baking tray. Bake for about 10-15 minutes, until golden brown. Cool on a wire rack.

Place the shortening, zest and chocolate in a bowl and warm in a bain-marie. Mix well until thoroughly melted.

Dip one half of each biscuit into the chocolate mixture. Alternatively, paint it on with a brush, making a decorative shape in the middle, or paint a 1 cm/½ in rim around the edge, etc.

DAPPLED LIGHT
The warmth of summer sunshine permeates every nook and cranny.

CHILLED SOUPS

Chilled Lebanese Soup

This and the three chilled soups which follow are ideal for making a day ahead and all benefit, in fact, from long chilling. This wonderfully refreshing cucumber and yoghurt soup is like a liquid salad.

Serves 6
Preparation: 20 mins, 24 hrs ahead

2 large cucumbers (with good green unblemished skins)
2 tbsp tarragon vinegar
2 garlic cloves, crushed
85 g/3 oz Greek yoghurt, lightly beaten
1 small carton (150 ml/¼ pt) single cream
300 ml/½ pt strong vegetable stock, cold
1 tbsp finely chopped gherkin
1 red onion, peeled and diced
115 g/4 oz peeled cooked prawns
salt and pepper
2 tbsp chopped parsley, to garnish

Wash the cucumbers, pat them dry and then grate them coarsely into a large mixing bowl. Add the vinegar and garlic and stir in the yoghurt, followed by the cream and then the stock.

Season well and mix in the mixed gherkin and onion. Chill in the refrigerator overnight. Just before serving, stir in the prawns, check seasoning and sprinkle over the chopped parsley.

Watercress Soup

This soup is equally delicious served chilled or hot.

Serves 8
Preparation: 10 mins
Cooking: 35 mins, 24 hrs ahead

2 large bunches of watercress
450 ml/¾ pt vegetable stock
45 g/1½ oz butter
1 large onion, peeled and chopped
30 g/1 oz flour
300 ml/½ pt milk
1 heaped tsp Dijon mustard
1 tsp tarragon vinegar
300 ml/½ pt single cream
salt and pepper

Wash the watercress thoroughly and cut it up, with the stalks, reserving the best leaves for garnish.

Put half of the watercress in a pan with the stock and 300 ml/½ pt water. Bring to the boil and then reduce the heat and simmer gently for 20 minutes. Remove from the heat and allow to cool.

Melt the butter in a pan and add the remaining watercress. Sauté gently for 5 minutes, add the onion and cook for about 5 minutes more.

Add the flour, then gradually add the milk, stirring constantly to make a white sauce. Simmer for a minute or two and then add the mustard and vinegar. Allow to cool.

Combine both watercress mixtures and purée in a blender. Add the cream, season well and put in the refrigerator until well chilled.

Serve the chilled soup garnished with the reserved watercress leaves.

Rich Minted Yoghurt Soup

Fresh mint leaves add tanginess to cream and Greek yoghurt. Use common garden or lemon mint if possible.

Serves 6
Preparation: 5 mins, 24 hrs ahead

575 ml/1 pt Greek yoghurt
300 ml/½ pt single cream
½ tsp roasted cumin seeds, ground
450 ml/¾ pt vegetable stock
1 tsp lemon juice
1 tsp lime juice
about 12 leaves of fresh mint
salt and pepper

Lightly whisk the yoghurt with a fork until creamy and smooth. Gradually beat in the cream, cumin seeds, stock and lemon and lime juices. Season well and then store the soup in the refrigerator until well chilled.

Just before serving, place the mint leaves on top of each other, roll them up and snip into fine shreds. Sprinkle these on the soup to serve.

Chilled Apricot Soup

Serves 8
Preparation: 20 mins, 24 hrs ahead

225 g/½ lb dried apricots
350 g/12 oz fresh apricots, stoned
85 g/3 oz caster sugar
850 ml/1½ pt dry white wine
juice and grated zest of ½ an
unwaxed lemon
juice and grated zest of ½ an unwaxed lime
300 ml/½ pt single cream, chilled
finely chopped parsley, to garnish

Use the fullest-fleshed dried apricots with not too wrinkled skins and reserve the 8 best-looking. Pour boiling water to cover over the others and leave to plump up. Discard the water and rinse the apricots in cold water.

Combine the fresh and dried apricots and in a blender purée to a fine pulp.

Dissolve the sugar in the white wine and add this to the apricot pulp. Blend again and then add the lemon and lime juices and zest. Store in the refrigerator until well chilled.

Swirl the cream into the soup and serve garnished with the parsley and the reserved apricots sliced very thinly.

Rich Minted Yoghurt Soup LEFT *(p. 55)*,
Watercress Soup CENTRE *(p. 55)*,
Chilled Apricot Soup RIGHT

VEGETABLES AND HERBS

Asparagus Tartlets

Makes 16 tartlets
Preparation: 20 mins
Cooking: about 20 mins

225 g/8 oz flour, sifted
½ tsp salt
150 g/5½ oz butter, softened
350 g/12 oz thin young fresh asparagus,
trimmed
8 eggs
150 ml/¼ pt double cream
salt
½ tsp freshly ground black pepper
iced water

Preheat the oven to 200C/400F/gas 6 and lightly grease sixteen 7·5 cm/3 in tartlet tins with a little butter.

Make the pastry: mix the flour with the salt in a bowl, then rub in 115 g/4 oz of the butter until the mixture has the consistency of fine breadcrumbs.

Stir in enough ice-cold water to make a soft, but not sticky, dough and roll this out on a floured surface to a thickness of about 3 mm/⅛ in. Cut out 16 circles of dough big enough to line the tartlet tins.

Prick the pastry cases all over, line with greaseproof paper and weight with baking beans. Bake blind for 10 minutes. Remove the beans and paper and bake again for a further 5 minutes until the pastry is light golden in colour.

Meanwhile, make the filling: steam the asparagus until just tender. Remove and reserve 32 good-looking tips. Mash the asparagus and warm gently in a dry pan.

Beat the eggs well and then mix in the cream. Season well with salt and the freshly ground black pepper.

Melt the remaining butter in a heavy-bottomed pan and place the egg mixture in the pan. Cook over a gentle heat, stirring constantly, until the mixture is just beginning to set but is still quite sloppy. Mix in the warmed asparagus and beat well with a wooden spoon.

Spoon the filling into the pastry cases, garnish each with 2 of the reserved asparagus tips crossed and serve:

Note: the pastry cases may be made ahead and stored in an airtight container until they are needed. Warm them through in a low oven before filling.

Herbed New Potatoes

Serves 6
Preparation: 15 mins
Cooking: about 20 mins

900 g/2 lb new potatoes
55 g/2 oz chopped fresh parsley
30 g/1 oz chopped fresh chives
30 g/1 oz chopped fresh coriander
85 g/3 oz butter
salt and pepper

Scrub the potatoes well and then plunge them into a large pan of boiling salted water. Cook for about 20 minutes, or until tender. Drain and keep warm.

Mix the herbs. Melt the butter in the bottom of a warmed serving dish and toss the herbs over that. Add the potatoes, season well and toss again until they are all covered with the herb butter.

Haricots Verts

WITH CAPER LEAF
VINAIGRETTE

Serves 4-6
Preparation: 15 mins
Cooking: 5 mins

1 small tin (115 g/4 oz) of caper leaves,
drained
675 g/1½ lb fine young haricots verts,
trimmed
rock salt
4 tbsp virgin olive oil
1 tbsp Japanese rice vinegar
1 tbsp crème fraîche
2 heaped tsp Dijon mustard
1 tbsp finely chopped capers
2 or 3 tbsp milk
salt and pepper

Carefully pick the caper leaves off the stalks. Discard the thorny stalks and chop the leaves roughly. Add some rock salt to a large pan of water, bring to the boil and plunge the beans into it. Stir for about 4 minutes, then drain the beans and refresh briefly under cold running water. Place in a warmed serving dish.

Mix together all the other ingredients, with the caper leaves, using the milk to dilute to a good coating consistency if necessary. Season the sauce to taste and pour over the beans.

FIELDS OF GREEN *(above right)*
Lush pastures beckon to leisurely picnics.

Summer Vegetables

CRISPLY SAUTÉED

Serves 6
Preparation: 20 mins
Cooking: about 5 mins

2 bunches of spring onions
3½ tbsp sesame oil
55 g/2 oz butter
15 g/½ oz rock salt
1 tsp freshly ground black pepper
30 g/1 oz finely grated unpeeled
fresh ginger

juice of 1 small lime
170 g/6 oz mange-tout peas, trimmed and
cut in half lengthwise
115 g/4 oz young carrots, cleaned and cut
into julienne strips
1½ large stalks of firm white celery,
trimmed and thinly sliced
115 g/4 oz fine green beans, trimmed
85 g/3 oz pumpkins seeds, dry roasted
1 tbsp chopped mixed parsley and chives,
to garnish

Cut the green tops from the spring onions; reserve. Slice the bulbs in half.

Heat the sesame oil and butter gently in a wok (or large sauté pan). Add the spring onions and half each of the salt, pepper, ginger and lime juice. Sauté gently until the onions are slightly translucent but not completely soft.

Increase the heat and add all the vegetables and stir and toss so that they are all well covered with the oil and butter mixture. Cook for 3-5 minutes, or until they are all tender but still firm.

Add the remaining salt, pepper, ginger and lime juice. Toss in the pumpkin seeds and stir to mix well. Transfer to a warmed serving dish and garnish generously with the chopped herbs and snipped spring onion tops.

Broad Beans

WITH PINE NUTS AND
BASIL SAUCE

Serves 8
Preparation: 20 mins
Cooking: about 10 mins

45 g / 1½ oz butter
55 g / 2 oz flour, sifted
575 ml / 1 pt milk
1 tsp Dijon mustard
1½ tsp Japanese rice vinegar
3 generous tbsp pesto sauce
3·5 k / 8 lb young tender broad beans, shelled
115 g / 4 oz pine nuts
10 basil leaves, snipped
salt and pepper

Melt the butter in a heavy-bottomed saucepan over a low heat. Add the flour and cook gently, stirring constantly, for about 3 minutes.

Remove the pan from the heat and gradually add one-third of the milk, stirring to combine it well. Return the pan to the heat and beat as the mixture thickens. Repeat this process until all the milk has been incorporated. Add the mustard, rice vinegar and pesto sauce, stirring gently to mix.

Cook the beans in lightly salted boiling water for 3 minutes. Drain and refresh briefly in cold water. Place in a warmed serving dish and cover with the pine nuts, reserving a few for garnish.

Pour the sauce over the beans and garnish with the snipped basil leaves and the remaining pine nuts.

FISH AND MEAT

Mange-Tout Peas

WITH PRAWNS AND
MOCK CAVIAR

Serves 6
Preparation: 15 mins
Cooking: 5 mins

900 g / 2 lb mange-tout peas, trimmed
350 g / 12 oz fresh (not frozen) peeled
cooked prawns, deveined
1½ tbsp crème fraîche
2 sprigs of dill, to garnish
10 borage flower heads

for the vinaigrette:
3 tbsp oil
1 tbsp vinegar
2 heaped tsp French mustard
juice of ½ a lemon
½ tsp sugar
1 small jar (115 g / 4 oz) of black mock
caviar
salt and pepper

Plunge the mange-tout peas into a pan of lightly salted boiling water and blanch for 2 minutes, stirring constantly. Drain and refresh the peas briefly under cold running water.

Summer Vegetables Crisply Sautéed
LEFT *(p.59), Broad Beans with Pine Nuts*
and Basil Sauce CENTRE, *Mange-Tout Peas*
with Prawns and Mock Caviar RIGHT

Place the peas in a glass serving dish or bowl and sprinkle over the prawns.

Make the vinaigrette using the oil, vinegar, mustard, lemon juice, sugar and salt and pepper to taste. Stir in the mock caviar, reserving a little for garnish.

Just before serving, dress the salad with the vinaigrette and toss gently. Place the crème fraîche on top in the middle and garnish that with the reserved mock caviar, dill and some of the borage. Sprinkle the remaining borage petals over the salad and serve immediately.

Note: if the salad is dressed too early, the mock caviar will stain the prawns.

Buckwheat Pancakes

WITH SMOKED EEL AND
SOUR CREAM

You could let guests help themselves to the pancake fillings.

Makes 20
Preparation: 15 mins, 2 hrs ahead
Cooking: about 40 mins

115 g / 4 oz buckwheat flour
115 g / 4 oz stoneground wholemeal flour
1 tsp salt
2 eggs, beaten
575 ml / 1 pt semi-skimmed milk
2 unwaxed lemons
2 unwaxed limes
2 bunches of spring onions
1 large carton (250 ml / 8 fl oz) sour cream
350 g / 12 oz smoked eel fillets, thinly sliced
sunflower margarine, for frying

Place the flours in a mixing bowl with the salt. Mix and create a well in the middle. Put the eggs in the well.

Using a balloon whisk in a rotating movement, gradually incorporate the milk into the mixture, gathering in the flours from the sides a little at a time until the batter is smooth and has a good pouring consistency (a little extra milk may be needed). Leave to stand for at least 2 hours.

Slice each lemon and lime into 12 wedges. Trim and clean the spring onions and then cut them (including the green leaves) into rings about 3 mm / ⅛ in thick and place in a bowl. Put the sour cream in a similar bowl.

Arrange the slices of smoked eel on a large serving plate and garnish with the lemon and lime wedges.

Melt a small quantity of the sunflower margarine in a pancake or small frying pan over a moderate heat. Pour in just enough batter to cover the bottom with a thin layer, tilting and swirling the pan as the batter goes in to coat the base.

Cook the pancake for a minute or so until small bubbles appear on the surface, then flip over and cook the other side. Turn out of the pan onto a warmed serving plate, cover with foil and keep warm in a low oven.

Cook all the pancakes in the same way and stack on the plate in the oven with a sheet of kitchen paper between each one. When they are all cooked, serve with the accompaniments. Place some sour cream on each pancake and then top this with a slice of eel and some spring onions. Season, squeeze over some lemon or lime juice and roll up the pancake into a cylinder.

Halibut Steaks

WITH SAMPHIRE

Serves 6
Preparation: 5 mins
Cooking: about 35 mins

6 halibut steaks, each weighing about
170 g/6 oz
125 ml/4 fl oz double cream
2 egg yolks
½ tsp cornflour
6 tbsp Noilly Prat
juice of ½ a lemon
juice of ½ a lime
salt and pepper
900 g/2 lb fresh samphire

Preheat the oven to 200C/400F/gas 6 and place the halibut steaks in a lightly oiled ovenproof dish.

Put the cream, egg yolks and cornflour into a bain-marie or double boiler over a gentle heat and stir constantly until the mixture thickens. Add the Noilly Prat, salt and pepper to taste and the lemon and lime juices.

Pour the sauce over the fish, cover with metal foil and bake for 20 minutes. At the end of this time, remove the foil, increase the oven temperature to 220C/425F/gas 7 and cook for a further 5 minutes. Remove the dish from the oven and keep hot.

Wash the samphire thoroughly and toss into a large pan of *unsalted* boiling water. Stir frequently for 2-3 minutes, then drain well and make nests of it on each of 6 warmed plates.

Place the steaks in the centre of each nest and serve the sauce separately.

Salmon

WITH FRESH GINGER AND
MUSTARD FLOWER SAUCE

If mustard flower heads are not available,
you can use other flower heads or herbs
for the garnish.

Serves 6
Preparation: 10 mins
Cooking: about 15 mins

6 fresh salmon cutlets, each weighing about
170 g/6 oz
1 bottle (700 ml/1¼ pt) dry white wine
1 tbsp grated peeled fresh ginger
salt and freshly ground black pepper

for the sauce:
300 ml/½ pt milk
2 tbsp mustard flower heads
1 tbsp butter
1 tsp English mustard powder
2 tbsp flour
½ tbsp white wine vinegar

First prepare the sauce ingredients: in a
small pan, heat the milk almost to boiling
point, put the mustard flower heads into
it, reserving 2 for garnish. Remove the
pan from the heat and leave to infuse for
10 minutes.

Season the salmon with the salt and
black pepper. Put the wine into a pan
with the ginger, bring to just below the
boil and add the fish. Cover and simmer
very gently for about 8 minutes.

Meanwhile, finish off the sauce: melt
the butter in a heavy-bottomed pan over
a low heat. Add the mustard powder and
the flour. Cook for 3 minutes, stirring
constantly. Add the vinegar and stir
slowly. Gradually add the flower heads
with the milk then bring the mixture to
the boil. Season and keep warm.

Remove the fish from the wine and
strain the ginger from the liquid (reserve
or freeze this for use as a fish stock).
Place the cutlets on a warm serving dish
and sprinkle with the ginger.

Cover the cutlets with the sauce,
garnish with the reserved flower heads
and serve.

Croissant Fillings

Although it is usually associated with
sweet things, virtually any filling and any
combination – including sweet and
savoury ones – can be used for the
versatile croissant pastry (see page 52).

Fills 12 croissants
Preparation: 15 mins
Cooking: 10 mins

6 rashers of smoked green back bacon
12 fresh prunes, stoned
12 dried apricots
55 g/2 oz butter
30 g/1 oz flour
150 ml/¼ pt milk
115 g/4 oz cooked smoked haddock, flaked
115 g/4 oz canned sweet corn, drained
salt and pepper

Grill the bacon, remove the rinds and
reserve the fat. Keep the grilled bacon
and the fat warm.

Pour some boiling water to cover the
prunes in one small dish and the apricots
in another. Leave to plump up, then
remove them from the water, pat dry and
chop both finely.

Toss the chopped prunes in the bacon
fat, stir to coat and remove. Do the same
with the chopped apricots and season
both to taste.

Melt the butter in a small pan and add
the flour. Cook thoroughly for a minute
or so, then gradually add the milk,
stirring constantly, and bring to the boil.
Simmer for 2 minutes, then adjust the
seasoning. Add the flaked haddock and
drained sweet corn and mix everything
together well (it should have a fairly
thick consistency).

Slit the croissants once slightly cool,
place a rasher of bacon in each of half of
them and then fill these with either
apricots or prunes. Stuff the others with
the fish mixture.

Serve while still hot.

Pork Fillet

WITH PURPLE SAGE BUTTER

Serves 4
Preparation: 10 mins
Cooking: about 20 mins

3 tbsp good quality vegetable oil
675 g/1½ lb pork fillet, cut into 1 cm/½ in
pieces
juice of 2 lemons
10 sage flower heads, to garnish

for the sage butter:
45 g/1½ oz butter
30 g/1 oz tender young sage leaves, chopped
1 tbsp lime juice
4 tbsp single cream
4 tbsp crème fraîche
salt and pepper

Heat the oil in a heavy-bottomed pan
over a moderate heat and stir-fry the
pork pieces until sealed, then add the
lemon juice.

Continue to stir-fry for about 8
minutes, until the meat is cooked
according to taste.

Transfer the well-drained pork pieces to a warmed serving dish. Cover and keep the dish warm while making the purple sage butter.

Melt the butter in a sauté pan over a moderate heat and sauté the sage leaves for 2 minutes. Add the lime juice and stir for about 30 seconds. Increase the heat to high and cook for a further 30 seconds.

Reduce the heat to low and add the cream, season to taste and then add the crème fraîche. Heat through but do not allow to boil.

To serve, pour the purple sage butter over the pork and garnish with the sage flower heads.

A TASTE OF HERBS
Rosemary, purple sage, chives and dill are attractive not only in their culinary potential – their delicate flowers and foliage make them look almost too good to eat.

Brick-Baked Lamb

WITH LAVENDER AND HAY

Serves 6
Preparation: 10 mins
Cooking: 20 mins per 450 g/1 lb for slightly
pink lamb, 25 mins for well-done

1 boned leg or loin of lamb, weighing about
1·8-2·3 k/4-5 lb.

about 24 heads and stalks of lavender

bunch of hay (dried grass), about
6 cm/2½ in across

115 g/4 oz butter

salt and pepper

Preheat the oven to 220C/425F/ gas 7.

Make 8 shallow incisions all over the surface of the lamb and insert a lavender head into each.

Wash the bunch of hay by holding under cold running water and then shake it lightly to dry it a little, but allow it still to retain some water. Bend the bunch of hay into a nest shape and place it inside an earthenware chicken brick. Sprinkle the remaining lavender over the hay, reserving a few of the best lavender sprigs for garnish.

Smear the lamb all over with the butter, then season generously. Place the lamb on the hay nest and push it down into the centre of it. Spoon 4 tablespoons of water over the lamb and then put the lid in place.

Bake for 20 minutes per 450 g/1 lb (for pink lamb, 25 minutes for well-done), removing the lid for the last 10 minutes of cooking. Transfer the cooked lamb to a warmed serving plate.

Carefully remove the hay from the brick, shaking off any juices back into the base. Strain the juices in the brick into a small saucepan. Bring to the boil; adjust the seasoning if necessary.

Serve the lamb garnished with some fresh sprigs of lavender, with the cooking juices in a warmed sauce boat or jug.

Brick-Baked Lamb with Lavender and Hay (left)

WILD LAVENDER *(above)*

FRUIT AND FLOWERS

Gooseberry Fool

If available, add one large head of elderflower when cooking the gooseberries, to counteract their acidity.

Serves 6
Preparation: 20 mins
Cooking: 10 mins
Chilling: 3 hrs

450 g / 1 lb ripe gooseberries
85 g / 3 oz caster sugar
85 g / 3 oz icing sugar
¾ tsp ground ginger
1 unwaxed orange
450 ml / ¾ pt double cream, lightly whipped

Top and tail the gooseberries, then rinse them but do not shake off all the water.

Put both sugars in 150 ml/¼ pt of water in a heavy-bottomed saucepan over a moderate heat, then add the berries. Bring to the boil, then simmer gently until the berries have cooked to a pulp and the water has reduced. Remove from the heat and allow to cool.

When cool, stir in the ginger then liquidize the pulp in a blender. To remove the pips, strain through a nylon sieve into a serving dish. Grate 1 tsp zest and squeeze 1 tsp juice from the orange. Add the zest and juice to the liquidized gooseberries and then fold in the cream. Chill for at least 3 hours.

Serve very cold, preferably with light ginger biscuits.

Marzipan Strawberries

Strawberries lend themselves particularly well to being transformed in this way because of their firmness and shape. Other soft fruit such as large loganberries or stoned cherries work well too.

Makes about 12-20
Preparation: 5 mins
Cooking: 20 mins, 4 days ahead

12-20 strawberries, depending on size (see below)
225 g / 8 oz good quality dark chocolate

Marzipan Strawberries LEFT, *Crystallized Petals and Flowers* RIGHT *(p.47) (above)*

COOL BLUES *(left)*

for the marzipan:
225 g/8 oz caster sugar
pinch of cream of tartar
225 g/8 oz ground almonds, sieved
½ tsp lemon juice
1 tsp triple-strength rose water (optional)
1 tsp red food colouring (optional)
1 tsp green food colouring (optional)
55 g/2 oz icing sugar, sifted

Make the marzipan 2 days in advance: put the sugar in 125 ml/4 fl oz water in a heavy-bottomed saucepan and bring to the boil, stirring well to dissolve all the sugar before the liquid actually comes to boiling point. Add the cream of tartar dissolved in a little water. Put a sugar thermometer in the pan and boil the mixture until it reaches a temperature of 116C/240F.

Remove from the heat and stir in the ground almonds (they must not be at all lumpy), lemon juice and rose water, if using. Form the paste into a bowl. If wishing to colour the paste, divide it into smaller balls and colour as desired.

Once the paste is cool, knead until smooth on a surface lightly dusted with sieved icing sugar.

Wrap with greaseproof paper, plastic film or metal foil, put in an airtight container and leave for 36 hours.

Choose firm full sweet-smelling strawberries of a uniform size, with the hull and stalk intact. The larger they are the fewer you will need (and have the marzipan to cover!). Wipe them clean with a slightly damp cloth.

Roll out the marzipan paste quite thinly, then cut it into enough 3·5 cm/1½ in (larger for big strawberries) squares, or circles if preferred, to cover all the strawberries. Mould each piece of marzipan around the pointed end of a strawberry furthest from the stalk, so that it comes about two-thirds of the way up the fruit.

Melt the chocolate in the top of a double boiler set over a gentle heat. When it is completely melted and still glossy, dip the strawberries into the chocolate to the level desired on the marzipan. Leave them to dry upside down on a rack.

Rosé and Rose Petal Sorbet

The heady fragrance of roses has made them a favourite ingredient, particularly in oriental sweets and pastries, throughout history. Use old-fashioned rose petals if possible – their scent is much stronger.

Serves 6
Preparation: 10 mins
Cooking: about 20 mins, 24 hrs ahead

3 tbsp triple-strength rose water
24 young pink and white heavy-scented rose petals (plus extra for garnish if desired)
200 g/7 oz caster sugar
450 ml/¾ pt rosé wine (Rosé d'Anjou, Blush or Lambrusco)
2 egg whites

Add the rose water to 150 ml/¼ pt of water and heat together in a pan until moderately hot.

If the rose petals are older, remove any white heel at their base with scissors. Blanch the rose petals in the liquid for 5 minutes, then refresh in cold water. Drain the petals carefully and pat dry on paper towels.

Put 170 g/6 oz of the sugar in a pan with 450 ml/¾ pt of water and heat slowly until the sugar dissolves completely. Then quickly bring the mixture to the boil, reduce the heat and simmer for 3 minutes. Remove from the heat and allow to cool.

Add the wine to this cooled syrup, mix and put in a suitable freezer container, cover and freeze until slushy, stirring from time to time.

Whisk the egg whites until stiff, then add the remaining caster sugar and whisk until completely blended. Add this mixture to the 'blush slush' and sprinkle in the blanched rose petals, distributing them as evenly as possible. Freeze again until firm.

Crystallize the remaining rose petals as described on page 47 and use them as garnish when serving the sorbet.

Note: for those with a sweet tooth, use the rose water to make up the 450 ml/¾ pt of water.

Hazelnut Roulade

WITH BLACKBERRIES AND LOGANBERRIES

If loganberries are not available, raspberries can be substituted.

Serves 6-8
Preparation: 30 mins
Cooking: 15 mins, plus filling and rolling

7 eggs, separated
200 g/7 oz caster sugar
2 tsp baking powder
170 g/6 oz ground dry hazelnuts
2 tbsp icing sugar, sifted
350 ml/12 fl oz double cream
285 g/10 oz ripe blackberries
285 g/10 oz ripe loganberries
1 tbsp Mur or cassis liqueur
sprigs of blackberry stem, to garnish (optional)

Preheat the oven to 180C/350F/gas 4. Oil a 27·5x43·5 cm/11 x 17 in sandwich tin and then line it with greaseproof paper (making sure it extends above the sides of the tin by at least 5 cm/2 in). Oil the paper lining.

Place the egg yolks in a blender and beat at moderate speed for 2 minutes. Gradually add the sugar and beat for at least 5 minutes, until the mixture is thick and creamy and ribbon trails will form on its surface.

In a bowl, add the baking powder to the hazelnuts, mix thoroughly and then add this to the egg mixture. Blend evenly at low speed.

Whisk the egg whites until they are just frothy and becoming firm. Add one-quarter of the egg whites to the nut mixture. Continue whisking the remaining egg whites until stiff and then fold them gently into the nut mixture with a metal spoon.

Spread the mixture into the prepared tin and bake for 15 minutes. Allow it to cool.

Remove the cooled cake from the tin, loosening the edges first. Place on the work surface 2 strips of greaseproof paper overlapping lengthwise to make a big enough base for the cake. Dust the paper with half the icing sugar. Invert the cake on the paper and remove the lining paper from its underside.

Whip the cream until stiff and then spread it over the cake. Sprinkle this with the fruit, reserving some of the best berries for garnish.

Using the paper to help, roll up the cake, starting from one short side. Transfer to a serving dish and decorate with the reserved fruit and the black-berry stems, if using. Spoon the liqueur over the fruit, dust with the remaining icing sugar and eat quickly.

THE PERFECTION OF ROSES
A simple arrangement of roses transforms a quiet corner.

Jewel Tart

WITH MARIGOLD CREAM

Serves 8
Preparation: 30 mins, 3 hrs ahead
Cooking: 45 mins

100 g/3½ oz redcurrants, destalked
55 g/2 oz white currants, destalked
55 g/2 oz blackcurrants, destalked
175 g/6½ oz redcurrant (or apricot) jelly

for the pâte sucrée:
200 g/7 oz flour
225 g/8 oz butter, cut into small pieces
85 g/3 oz icing sugar, sifted
pinch of salt
2 egg yolks

for the marigold cream:
575 ml/1 pt double cream
140 g/5 oz caster sugar
4 eggs
3 drops of vanilla essence
petals from 2 heads of calendula

First of all make the pâte sucrée: place the flour on a cool working surface (preferably marble) and make a well in the middle.

Put the butter in the well. Work the butter with the fingertips until softened and then add in the sugar and salt, mixing in thoroughly. Then gradually add the egg yolks.

At this point start drawing in the flour from the sides, mixing well each time, until all is combined.

Work the dough with the palm of the hand until it is even and smooth. Roll the dough into a ball, cover and chill for a few hours.

When well chilled, preheat the oven to 220C/425F/gas 7. Roll out the dough to line a greased 22·5 cm/8½ in round baking tin. Bake the pastry blind (using beans or rice) for 15 minutes. (Any surplus pastry will freeze well.)

Meanwhile make the marigold cream: in a bowl mix the cream, sugar and eggs and whisk them together. Add the vanilla and the petals.

When the pastry case is cooked, remove it from the oven and reduce the oven temperature to 180C/350F/gas 4. Pour the marigold cream into the pastry case and cook for a further 25-30 minutes, or until the cream sets. Remove from the oven.

Melt the jelly in a small pan and allow to cool slightly.

Discard any bruised or damaged fruit, rinse in cold water, shake well and pat dry on paper towels. Scatter the berries to cover the cream mixture completely, then glaze the top with the jelly to serve.

Note: one good way of destalking currants is to pull the prongs of a fork through them.

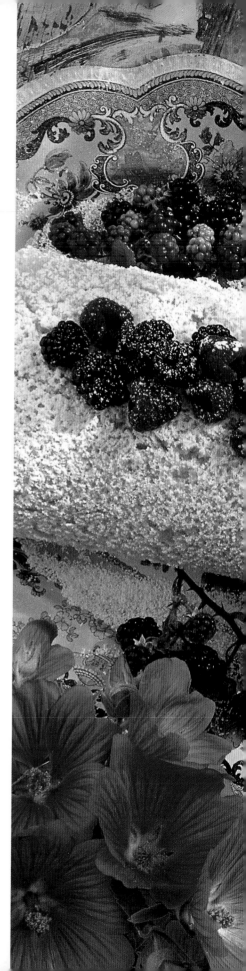

Hazelnut Roulade with Blackberries and Loganberries LEFT *(p.71),*
Jewel Tart with Marigold Cream RIGHT

Autumn

THE GLORY OF THE HARVEST

Autumn is throwing on her mantle, a gentle riot of colour spanning the spectrum
of the artist's palette – pale lime to deep evergreen, copper through to
crimson, scarlet and flame, spruce blue and chocolate brown, honey yellow to
pear gold and burnt orange. Plump, rosy red apples, quince,
misty blue sloes and fat blackberries ache to part company from their life force,
tumbling to the ground. Those that escape the eyes and mouths of birds,
insects and animals rest untouched to begin again the cycle of
regeneration. Golden sweet corn, curly kale, pumpkins, hazel and cob nuts are all
gathered in at harvest time to decorate our churches and tables, to be
turned then into nourishing food to soothe bodies that are
becoming chillier daily.

AUTUMN MIST (*above*)

FROSTY HEDGEROWS (*previous page*)

Country roads bustle with mechanical life and all the business of hedge-trimming, ditch-clearing, ploughing and seeding – sadly, too, spraying. The farming community works against the quickly falling darkness, tending early calves and lambs with a tender eye towards the biting east wind and cold frosty mornings bound to arrive at any time. Squirrels are desperately hoarding walnuts, cobs, sweet chestnuts and acorns. Few escape their beady eyes as they dash from hiding place to hiding place, their ceaseless efforts occupying them from dawn to dark.

Dawn greets us on these cool mornings with the cackling of the crow. Gone is the symphony of summer birdsong – only the resilient little robin sings his heart out through the day. The chaotic chorus of starlings circling in their flock as they search for their bed-time resting place is one of the last sounds as night begins to fall.

With wild plants, grasses and flowers at the end of their natural life-cycle, collecting seeds is useful. Arm yourself with envelopes and a felt tip pen and crumble the seeds into an envelope per plant. Label and leave them to dry thoroughly, until planting time in the spring. It brings a real sense of achievement when they appear in your chosen spot. Let children, under supervision, cut wild reed to adorn their own space. Over a six-week period, this beautiful reed changes from black to fluffy white, and, provided it is not moved constantly, will not shed all over the house.

The harvest is the climax of the farming year, and communities throughout the land celebrate this much-loved festival. Pumpkins give delighted children endless hours of pleasure. Traditional, of course, is the Hallowe'en face lit from within with a night-light. The seeds which have been removed can be put to good use in the form of jewellery collages or used to make pictures and bookmarks. The flesh of the pumpkin can go into soups and pies. Marrows and squashes can be baked whole or stuffed with fillings.

Wood-burning stoves, Agas and log fires spring back to life after their summer recess, and their smells bring delicious promises of the time to be spent in the warmth of the home and the kitchen. The smell of roasting chestnuts is something not to be missed, especially when snuggled close to an open fire listening to them hiss and pop. Sloes are gathered for the Christmas feasting to come; pears and apples are spiced, bottled and preserved, and made into delicious jams and jellies. Blackberries are picked for eating on their own, in pies

and to make prickle jam, and another beautiful hedgerow fruit, the versatile elderflower berry, makes wonderful wine, cordial and punch.

Big baking potatoes, broccoli and chestnuts, parsnips and pumpkin will be made into nutritious foods so that we can brace ourselves for the possibility of snow, sleet and cold, freezing fog. Cauliflowers, courgettes, onions and tomatoes are usually in plentiful supply at this time of year. Pickling is a delicious home-cooking event that can be shared by several enthusiasts around the kitchen table, and presents of fresh pickles are always received with great delight.

Native oysters, mussels and scallops, when bought fresh and eaten quickly, can be simply exquisite. Mackerel pâté, soused herring and whitebait all make excellent, easy-to-prepare starters.

Delicious – and deadly – fungi appear in woodlands, fields and sandy spots. Blewits, shaggy ink caps, parasols, field and horse mushrooms, chanterelles, puff balls, and oyster mushrooms can all be found (although once a location is discovered, it is jealously guarded). Positive identification, however, is an absolute must, and hand-washing after picking fundamental.

Game comes into its own during autumn. Roasts, casseroles and soups take on their own rich flavours, and make a change from the traditional Sunday joint. Pâtés also benefit from these special birds and animals. Make plaited loaves and fishes, wheat sheaves and mice, inspired by the joyous harvest festival celebrations being held in tiny churches everywhere.

As a novel idea for nibbles, pickle radish and mooli, red cabbage and celery Japanese-style in 13 parts salt to 1 part water. Leave for 5 days before eating. These pickled vegetables make an interesting alternative to peanuts and crisps.

Purple garlic stripped of outer leaves and drowned in virgin olive oil makes a delicate dressing oil. Make *pilli pilli ho ho* with fresh chillies and use a few splashes to excite a bland soup or stew. Put fresh green and red chillies into a long-necked bottle, then fill it to the top with whisky. Leave for a week and shake the bottle before use. When it is empty, fill it a second time with vodka. You can continue like this, always keeping the same chillies but alternating the spirit each time.

Green walnuts can be picked and pickled, whole almonds toasted, salted and kept for special aperitif times. Root vegetables can be eaten with gusto after months of crisp summer salads, and clementines bottled in Cointreau make a surprise dessert after a light meal.

Crab apple and Japonica quince make fragrant and subtle jellies and fresh cranberries are readily available. Make delicious fresh cranberry sauce, maybe adding port or brandy, to enjoy with Christmas fare, and now is the time to do battle with the birds for plump blue sloes to make that unmissable treat, sloe gin.

Sloe Gin

Makes two 750 ml/27 fl oz bottles

sloes (see below)
55 g/2 oz barley sugar, crushed
115 g/4 oz flaked almonds
1 bottle (750 ml/27 fl oz) gin

When picking the sloes, take 2 bottles and half fill each with the fruit.

Wash the sloes, then prick each of them with a fork and return them to the dry sterilized bottles.

To each bottle add half the barley sugar and half the almonds. Fill each bottle right to the top with the gin and cork or screw firmly.

Leave to stand, at room temperature, for at least 12 weeks, turning several times to keep the sugar dissolved and redistribute the almonds.

Serve straight from the bottle, allowing one or two of the sloes into each glass. This is a potent drink, so enjoy carefully!

Orange pomanders take about six weeks to become hard, so now is the time to start making them. They can then be ready for Christmas presents or decorations, or simply to hang in cupboards or to lay in drawers.

Orange Pomanders

1 strip of bias binding or plain tape, about
30 cm/1 ft long
cocktail stick
2 unwaxed oranges
55 g/2 oz whole cloves
15 g/½ oz ground orris root
2 strips of pretty ribbon, about
32·5 cm/18 in long and 6 mm/¼ in wide

Pin the binding or tape symmetrically around the two axes of each orange to divide them into four quarters.

Make holes with the cocktail stick and push the pointed ends of the cloves into the skins of the oranges to cover the bare quarters. Leave enough space between them to allow for the skin shrinking as the oranges dry.

Remove the binding or tape, put the oranges in a bowl and sprinkle them with the ground orris root. Tie the oranges with string and hang them from a coat hanger in a warm room (not an airing cupboard or kitchen as these are too hot). Leave them for six weeks, turning them upside down every 2 days or so (so that the juice flows and the skin does not rot) until they are hard.

Brush off the surplus orris root and tie the coloured ribbons over where the tape lay, finishing with a pretty bow on top.

Summery blue skies have changed and the colours are more turquoise. Blustery winds and short, sharp bursts of rainfall leave cloud formations a phenomenon to behold – prehistoric monsters, cotton wool characters, toast rack stripes and whole lands of gloriously designed futuristic buildings sail past on the autumn winds in a constantly changing panorama.

MENUS *for Autumn*

BREAKFAST
Marrow and Ginger Compote (p. 82)
Granary Bread with Grilled Brie (p. 87)
Brioches with Quince and Medlar Preserve
(p. 80)
Chanterelle Omelette (p. 88)

LIGHT LUNCH
Calabrese Soufflé (p. 92)
Gooey Meringue with Greengages (p. 99)
Almond Tuiles (p. 82)

LUNCH
Oyster Mushrooms Provençale (p. 88)
Chicken and Paprika Casserole (p. 93)
Pear and Stilton Strudel (p. 97)
Great Aunt Sybil's Apple Crunch (p. 97)

TEA
Carob Fingers (p. 83)
Rosemary and Sultana Buns (p. 82)
Elderberry and Blackberry Jam (p. 80)
Moist Carrot Cake (p. 85)

LIGHT SUPPER
Roast Quail with Watercress and
Ginger Wine (p. 93)
Vegetable Julienne with Orange Glaze
(p. 90)
Chestnuts in Syrup (p. 87)

DINNER
Pumpkin Soup with Garlic Croûtons
(p. 90)
Wild Duck with Nectarines and
Red Grapes (p. 96)
or
Guinea Fowl with Celery and Apple
(p. 94)
Glazed Parsnips (p. 92)
Profiteroles with Chocolate and
Violet Cream Sauce (p. 100)

HARVEST TREATS
*Pumpkins, preserved fruits and candlelight promise autumn
feasts in store.*

PREPARATION

Individual Brioches

Makes 12
Preparation: 30 mins, plus 1½ hrs rising
Cooking: 20 mins, plus cooling

15 g/½ oz dried yeast or
25 g/¾ oz fresh yeast
2½ tbsp sugar
125 ml/4 fl oz warm water
620 g/1 lb 6 oz plain flour, sifted
1 tsp salt
4 eggs, beaten + 1 extra yolk, beaten
185 g/6¾ oz butter, softened
3 tbsp cream

Place the yeast and 1 teaspoon of sugar in a bowl. (Omit the sugar if using fresh yeast.) Add the warm water, stir gently and leave in a warm place until the mixture becomes frothy.

Mix the remaining sugar with the flour and salt in a bowl. Make a well in the centre and add the 4 eggs and the yeast mixture. Gradually incorporate the flour from the edges and mix to a smooth dough. Remove the dough from the bowl and place on a lightly floured surface. Knead for 5 minutes, or until the dough becomes elastic and feels dry.

Work the softened butter into the dough gradually, a few pieces at a time. Knead again for about 10 minutes, until the dough is very elastic and shiny. Place the dough in a lightly greased bowl and leave to rise for about 1 hour, until it has almost doubled in size.

Remove the dough from the bowl, knock the air out and knead again until smooth. Divide into 12 pieces.

Preheat the oven to 200C/400F/gas 6 and grease 12 individual brioche moulds with butter.

Fill the moulds with the pieces of dough: first remove one-quarter of each piece and then mould the remaining piece into a ball and place this in the mould. Shape the smaller piece into a ball and place this on top of the larger ball. Brush all over with a mixture of beaten egg yolk and cream. Using a wooden skewer, push the dough from the top portion down to the lower portion during cooking.

Glaze again and allow to stand in a warm place for at least 15 minutes, until the dough pieces have doubled in size.

Bake for about 10 minutes, then reduce the heat to 180C/350F/gas 4 and bake for another 10 minutes until the brioches are golden brown and sound hollow when tapped.

Remove from the oven, take out of the mould and allow to cool on a wire rack. (Remove the tops if required for filling.)

Quince and Medlar Preserve

The delightfully old-fashioned medlar is a rare fruit nowadays and medlar trees are found only in well-established gardens. The medlar's delicate flavour, however, makes it well worth the effort of tracking it down.

Makes about 900 g/2 lb
Preparation: 30 mins
Cooking: 20 mins, plus cooling

7 quinces
7 medlars
juice and grated zest of 4 unwaxed oranges
juice and grated zest of 1 unwaxed lemon
1 stick of cinnamon, broken into 2 or 3 pieces
1·1 k/2½ lb sugar

Peel and core the quinces and cut them into coarse chunks. Peel the medlars and cover both with cold water in a large pan. Make sure *all* the pips are removed before cooking.

Bring the pan to the boil and then simmer gently until the fruit is tender. Drain and leave to cool.

When cool, purée in a blender and return to the rinsed-out pan. Add the fruit zest and juice, the cinnamon and the sugar. Mix well, bring to the boil and boil rapidly for about 10 minutes until the mixture starts to set.

Remove the cinnamon pieces and pour into warm dry sterilized glass containers and cover. Label.

Elderberry and Blackberry Jam

This rich, beautifully coloured jam keeps well for at least a year.

Preparation: 30 mins
Cooking: 40 mins, plus cooling

equal weights of blackberries and elderberries, washed and stalks removed
preserving sugar

Weigh the fruit and then put it in a preserving pan.

Using both hands, squeeze all the fruit gently. (The colour does stain the hands, but it is quite harmless and wears off eventually!) Slowly bring to the boil, stirring the fruit constantly, then keep boiling for 20 minutes.

Meanwhile, for each 450 g/1 lb of fruit,

measure out 350 g/12 oz of preserving sugar and warm briefly in the oven (this speeds the process).

Add the sugar to the pan at the end of the 20 minutes, mix thoroughly, bring back to the boil and boil again for another 20 minutes or until setting point is reached.

Pour the jam into warmed dry sterilized jars and cover while still hot.

Individual Brioches, Quince and Medlar Preserve

Marrow and Ginger Compote

Makes about 1·35 k/3 lb
Preparation: 30 mins, 24 hrs ahead
Cooking: 30 mins, plus cooling

1 ripe green vegetable marrow, weighing about 900 g/2 lb
900 g/2 lb preserving sugar
30 g/1 oz ground ginger
30 g/1 oz fresh ginger root, peeled
1½ large unwaxed lemons
½ tsp cayenne

Peel the marrow with a potato peeler, cut it in half, remove the seeds and cut the flesh into 5 x 2·5 cm/2 x 1 in chunks.

Place on the bottom of a deep bowl and sprinkle with half the sugar, the ground and fresh ginger, the rind of the half lemon cut into julienne strips (leaving the white pith on), the juice of all the lemon and the cayenne. Cover and leave for 24 hours.

Put a preserving pan over a moderate heat and put the marrow mixture into it. Cook gently until tender. Add the rest of the sugar and bring very, very slowly just to a simmer, stirring constantly. Cook gently until setting point is reached.

Mash the marrow with a potato masher, then pot in warm dry sterile pots. Cover and label.

Rosemary and Sultana Buns

Makes 12
Preparation: 20 mins, plus 45 mins proving
Cooking: 15-20 mins

250 ml/8 fl oz warm spring water
15 g/½ oz dried yeast
1½ tsp clear honey
2 tbsp wheatgerm
225 g/8 oz plain flour
170 g/6 oz 100% wholemeal flour
pinch of salt
1 tsp dried crushed rosemary
85 g/3 oz plump sultanas (unsulphured)
corn oil, for greasing
semolina, for dusting

for the glaze:
2 tbsp corn and barley malt
or
1 egg yolk, beaten
¼ tsp salt

Lightly oil a large mixing bowl and a baking tray. Sprinkle the latter with semolina and warm another bowl in the oven briefly.

Place the warm water in the warm bowl and sprinkle the yeast on top. Stir in the honey and wait until the mixture becomes spongy. Add the wheatgerm and the flours, salt, rosemary and sultanas. Stir lightly to form a dough.

Transfer the dough to the oiled bowl and knead it thoroughly for about 3 minutes. Leave in the bowl, cover with linen or cotton cloth and allow to rise in a warm place until the dough has about doubled in size.

Using the fist, punch the dough to release the air in it, then turn it out into a floured bowl and leave to rest for about 5 minutes. Separate the dough into 12 pieces and form them into balls.

Place the balls on the prepared tray, cut a cross indent on the top of each and glaze with the corn and barley malt or the egg mixed with the salt.

Allow to rise again for about 20-30 minutes. Preheat the oven to 200C/ 400F/gas 6 and bake for about 15-20 minutes in the middle of the oven.

Serve plain with butter, or with home-made jam.

Almond Tuiles

Makes about 14
Preparation: 8 mins
Cooking: 5 mins

white of 1 egg
55 g/2 oz caster sugar
2 tbsp plain flour, sifted
30 g/1 oz melted butter
½ tsp vanilla essence
55 g/2 oz chopped flaked almonds

Preheat the oven to 180C/350F/gas 4 and lightly grease a baking tray.

Beat the egg white to stiff peaks. Then slowly add the sugar a little at a time, beating well after each addition until the mixture is smooth.

Stir in the flour, followed by the melted butter and then the vanilla essence. Mix well.

Place a generous teaspoonful of the mixture on the prepared tray. Flatten each with the back of the spoon to make circles about 5 cm/2 in across. Sprinkle each lightly with the almonds.

Bake for about 5 minutes, until lightly brown around the edges.

Remove the tray from the oven, lift each tuile quickly off with a spatula and place around a clean rolling pin or narrow bottle. Press the sides gently to mould it into shape. Remove when cool and crisp.

Continue cooking in batches until all the mixture is used. The tuiles store well in airtight containers.

Carob Fingers

Makes about 24
Preparation: 10 mins
Cooking: 10 mins, 3 hrs ahead

115 g/4 oz each of sesame, sunflower, and
green pumpkin seeds
55 g/2 oz plump dry sultanas
4 puffed rice cakes, crumbled
½ tsp fine sea salt
3 tbsp corn and barley malt
1 packet (200 g/7 oz) pure creamed coconut
45 g/1½ oz carob powder
corn oil, for greasing

Preheat the oven to 180C/350F/gas 4. Spread the seeds out evenly on baking trays and roast for 10-15 minutes, shaking the trays occasionally and being careful not to overcook them. Grease a rectangular 17·5 x 27·5 cm/7 x 11 in baking tray with oil.

Place all the seeds and the sultanas in a heavy pan and sprinkle over the crumbled rice cakes and salt. Add the corn and barley malt and mix everything well together.

Gently warm over a moderate heat and stir again. The mixture should stick to the spoon quite firmly. If necessary, add more malt but make sure the mixture does not become too runny.

Place on the tray, pressing down firmly all over to an even thickness. Bake for 5-6 minutes *only*, until golden.

Melt the creamed coconut in a pan over a low heat, then stir in the carob powder. Allow to cool a little. When the mixture is cool, pour it over the baked seeds and smooth with a spatula.

Chill for about 30 minutes, then mark out 24 finger shapes on the surface. Chill again for at least 2 hours, or until needed. To serve, slice as required.

GOLDEN SUNFLOWERS AND ORANGES
(below)

Moist Carrot Cake (p. 85) *(overleaf)*

Moist Carrot Cake

Serves 10
Preparation: 15 mins
Cooking: 1 hr, plus cooling and frosting

275 ml/9 fl oz sunflower or vegetable oil
350 g/12 oz granulated sugar
4 eggs, well beaten
400 g/14 oz carrots, grated
225 g/8 oz unbleached self-raising flour
170 g/6 oz raisins
115 g/4 oz Brazil nuts, chopped
1 tsp ground cinnamon
1 tsp ground allspice
½ tsp ground nutmeg
½ tsp fine sea salt
6 drops of vanilla essence

for the frosting:
225 g/8 oz cream cheese
170 g/6 oz icing sugar, sifted
2 heaped tsp grated zest from orange

Preheat the oven to 160C/325F/gas 3. Put a circle of greaseproof paper in the bottoms of two 22·5 cm/9 in sandwich tins. Grease lightly and dust with sugar.

Place the oil and sugar in a blender and combine until smooth. Add the eggs and carrots and combine well again.

Place all the remaining dry ingredients, except the nuts and raisins, in a bowl, mix well and then gradually add this to the carrot mixture. Finally, add the nuts and raisins along with the vanilla.

Divide the mixture between the 2 prepared sandwich tins and bake them for about 1 hour, until golden. Remove from the oven and leave to cool slightly.

Make the frosting: cream the cheese with the sugar and orange zest. Spread half the mixture on top of each sponge then put one cake on top of the other.

WOODS AND FIELDS

Chestnuts in Syrup

These nuts in a cognac-flavoured syrup are a delightful gift. They also make a lovely light dessert after a rich meal and the syrup is actually good by itself, poured over ice cream, sorbet or fruit.

Fills three 450 g/1 lb jars
Preparation: 10 mins, 2 days ahead
Cooking: about 15 mins, several days ahead

450 g/1 lb fresh chestnuts
juice of 3 lemons
675 g/1½ lb granulated sugar
¾ tsp cream of tartar
100 ml/3½ fl oz cognac

Snip the tops off the chestnuts and place them in boiling water, a few at a time, for 2-3 minutes. Peel them carefully and remove the brown inner skin. Place the chestnuts in a bowl, cover with cold water, add the lemon juice and leave to soak overnight.

Drain, then plunge the chestnuts into a pan of boiling water. Simmer until tender but still firm.

Put the sugar and cream of tartar in 757 ml/1 pt of water in a pan and then allow the sugar to dissolve slowly over a gentle heat.

Drop the cooked nuts into the syrup and simmer for 10 minutes. Remove from the heat and leave to stand, covered, for 24 hours.

Next day, remove the nuts from the syrup with a slotted spoon. Put the syrup back on a high heat and bring to a fast boil. Leave to boil until it thickens to a honey-like consistency.

Place 2 tablespoons of cognac in each of 3 warmed dry sterilized glass jam jars. Put the chestnuts in the jars. Fill the jars with syrup and seal while still warm. Immediately turn upside down to mix in the cognac. Label and enjoy later.

Granary Bread

WITH GRILLED BRIE

Although bulghar – crushed wheat grains which have been partially cooked – is often called cracked wheat, you should use the form of cracked wheat also known as kibbled wheat for this recipe. This latter is uncooked crushed wheat grains and will result in a lighter bread than bulghar.

Makes two 450 g/1 lb loaves
Preparation: 10 mins, plus 45 mins proving
Cooking: 20-30 mins, plus cooling

55 g/2 oz rye flour
450 g/1 lb 100% stoneground wholemeal flour
1 tsp fine sea salt
115 g/4 oz cracked (kibbled) wheat
about 450 ml/¾ pt warmed spring water
15 g/½ oz fresh yeast or 30 g/1 oz dried yeast
1 tsp soft brown sugar
30 g/1 oz black treacle
225 g/8 oz fairly ripe Brie, cut into 6 mm/¼ in slices
1 tbsp roasted sunflower seeds (see page 83)

Preheat the oven to 200C/400F/gas 6 and grease two 450 g/1 lb loaf tins.

In a large mixing bowl, blend the flours with the sea salt and the cracked wheat, reserving 2 tablespoons of grain to decorate the loaves.

Warm a small bowl and put 150 ml/ ¼ pt of warm water in it with the yeast, adding the sugar if using dried yeast. Leave in a warm part of the kitchen for about 10 minutes until frothy. Pour into the flour mixture and then gradually blend in the rest of the warm water. Using the hands, mix thoroughly.

Divide the mixture into two and place each in a warmed prepared loaf tin. Cover with a clean damp linen cloth and leave to rise at room temperature until it is just above the top of the tin.

Bake in the middle of the oven for about 20 minutes. Remove from the oven and paint with the treacle while still hot. Coat with reserved cracked wheat grains.

Turn out on a wire rack to cool. Cut the cooled loaf into slices, toast one side and put a slice of Brie on untoasted side. Return to the grill and toast until the cheese bubbles and turns golden. Sprinkle with the sunflower seeds and allow to cool slightly.

Cut each slice into 4 or 8 pieces and serve as party finger food or with drinks.

HARVEST FIELDS
Autumn is a time of intense activity in the farming community, as the year's hard work comes to fruition.

Chanterelle Omelette

WITH CORIANDER

Serves 6 (makes 2 omelettes)
Preparation: 20 mins
Cooking: 5-8 mins

675 g / 1½ lb chanterelle mushrooms
10 eggs
2½ tbsp olive oil
10 spring onions, cleaned, trimmed and
roughly chopped (stalks included)
juice of 1 fresh lime
½ tsp dried ground coriander
85 g / 3 oz unsalted butter
1 tbsp freshly chopped coriander
sea salt and freshly ground black pepper

Remove the stems from the mushrooms, cutting off the small hard piece at the base, and reserve the heads and stems. Wash carefully, dry and chop finely.

Put the oil in a heavy pan over a moderate heat and add the onions, lime juice and dried coriander. Sauté gently for a few minutes. When tender but still crunchy, drain off the liquid and keep the onions warm in a bowl. Add two-thirds of the butter to the pan and toss in the mushrooms. Sauté until softened. Drain off any liquid and add the mushrooms to the bowl.

Beat 5 eggs with 1½ tablespoons of water until light and frothy. Add half of the remaining butter to a large frying pan. When melted and bubbling add the eggs to the pan.

Cook gently over a moderate heat, lifting the sides from time to time to watch for burning. While the middle of the mixture is still runny, add half of the mixture contents of the bowl. Season and add half the fresh coriander. Gently flip one side of the omelette over the filling.

Turn the omelette out on a warmed plate, flipping it over to cover the seam. Serve immediately.

Make a second omelette the same way.

Oyster Mushrooms Provençale

Serves 4
Preparation: 10 mins
Cooking: about 25 mins

3 tbsp virgin olive oil
2 garlic cloves, peeled and chopped
(not crushed)
2 onions, peeled and coarsely chopped
350 g / 12 oz beef tomatoes, blanched, peeled
and deseeded
2 heaped tsp herbes de Provence
350 g / 12 oz wild oyster mushrooms
250 ml / 8 fl oz dry white wine
1 tsp red wine vinegar
2 tbsp roughly chopped parsley
silverweed leaves, to garnish (optional)

Place the oil in a heavy-bottomed pan over a moderate heat. Add first the garlic, followed by the onion, then the tomatoes and finally the herbs, sautéing well for about 3 minutes each.

Increase the heat to high, add the mushrooms and stir constantly to coat all the ingredients well in oil.

Add the wine and vinegar and allow to bubble for about 2 minutes. Reduce the heat and allow to simmer for about 10 minutes. Remove from the heat. Add the parsley, transfer to a warmed serving dish and serve immediately, garnished with the silverweed leaves, if using.

Oyster Mushrooms Provençale LEFT,
Chanterelle Omelette with Coriander RIGHT

VEGETABLES

Vegetable Julienne

WITH ORANGE GLAZE

This julienne is time-consuming to prepare, unless your food processor can perform this function, but the vegetables look and taste so good that it is worth persevering.

Serves 6
Preparation: 15 mins
Cooking: 5 mins

8 slim carrots
8 slim courgettes
3 small turnips
4 slim parsnips
bunch of spring onions
30 g/1 oz butter
15 g/½ oz olive oil
½ tsp brown sugar
1 tbsp fresh orange juice
chopped parsley, to garnish

Wash and trim all the vegetables and then cut them into julienne strips, reserving the spring onion tops for the garnish.

Put the butter with the oil in a heavy-bottomed frying pan over a moderate heat. Add the sugar then toss in all the vegetables. Stir-fry quickly for about 2 minutes.

Turn up the heat to high and pour in the orange juice. Cook for a further 1 minute, coating all the vegetables evenly.

Transfer to a warmed serving dish and garnish with the snipped spring onion tops and the parsley.

Pumpkin Soup

Golden orange pumpkins are surely the quintessential autumn vegetables – and pumpkin soup one of the most delicious ways of using them.

Serves 4-6
Preparation: 15 mins
Cooking: 15 mins

1·35 k/3 lb pumpkin, peeled and cut into chunks
225 g/8 oz potatoes, peeled and cut into chunks
170 g/6 oz onions, chopped
55 g/2 oz butter
450 ml/¾ pt milk
1 tbsp flour
½ tsp freshly grated nutmeg
1 carton (250 ml/8 fl oz) single cream
salt and pepper

Put the pumpkin and potatoes in a large pan of boiling salted water and simmer until just tender. Drain, reserving the stock, and purée in an electric blender. Sieve, if necessary.

Sauté the onions lightly in a little of the butter in a pan over a moderate heat. Liquidize in the blender and add to the pumpkin and potato purée.

Bring 150 ml/¼ pt of the milk to the boil in a pan and melt the remaining butter in another. Add the flour to the butter and cook over a moderate heat for about 5 minutes, stirring constantly, until smooth. Add the nutmeg and a pinch of pepper.

Pour in the milk, a little at a time, stirring constantly. Then add the purée. Bring to the boil and then allow to simmer gently for 5 minutes. Remove from the heat and allow to cool.

Add 450 ml/¾ pt of the reserved stock. Return to the blender and purée again. Put back in the saucepan with the remaining milk and the cream and heat gently. Do *not* allow to boil! Serve immediately.

Garlic Croûtons

Serves 6
Preparation: 10 mins
Cooking: 10 mins

55 g/2 oz butter
55 g/2 oz vegetable oil
3 garlic cloves, peeled and finely chopped
4 large slices of brown or white bread, cut into small chunks (with crusts)

Melt the butter with the oil in a frying pan set over a moderate heat. Add the garlic and cook slowly until just golden.

Toss in the pieces of bread, turn up the heat to high and cook, stirring constantly, until the croûtons are all well covered in garlic and oil and are also a golden colour.

Drain on paper towels, if wished, and serve in, or to accompany, soup.

Vegetable Julienne with Orange Glaze LEFT,
Pumpkin Soup with Garlic Croûtons RIGHT

Glazed Parsnips

Serves 6
Preparation: 20 mins
Cooking: 30 mins

12 large parsnips
1 tsp rock salt
1 tbsp corn or olive oil
1 tbsp juice and 1 tbsp zest from 1 orange
1½ tbsp light brown sugar
1 tbsp soya sauce

Preheat the oven to 230C/450F/gas 8. Wash the parsnips, but do not peel them. Top and tail as necessary. Place in a large pan of boiling water with the rock salt. Boil for 10 minutes.

Put the remaining ingredients in a large flameproof dish. Place over a moderate heat and stir well.

Drain the parsnips, cut in half then roll them in the glaze. Bake in the oven for 20 minutes, turning once.

Calabrese Soufflé

Serves 8
Preparation: 10 mins
Cooking: about 40 mins

225 g/8 oz calabrese, washed and trimmed
85 g/3 oz unsalted butter
2 tbsp flour
300 ml/½ pt milk
6 eggs, separated
cayenne pepper
115 g/4 oz freshly grated Parmesan
1 tsp freshly grated nutmeg
salt

Preheat the oven to 190C/375F/gas 5 and generously grease a 1·75-2·2 l/3-4 pt soufflé dish with some butter.

Steam the calabrese until tender but still quite crunchy. Allow to cool a little and then chop into small pieces.

Melt the butter in a heavy-bottomed pan over a low heat. Add the flour and turn up the heat a little. Stir constantly over a moderate heat for at least 1 minute. Slowly add the milk and stir until the mixture thickens. Beat the egg yolks into the sauce one at a time. Stir in the calabrese, a pinch of cayenne, the nutmeg and the Parmesan. Season to taste with salt.

Whisk the egg whites to stiff peaks, then fold gently into the sauce. Quickly turn the mixture into the prepared soufflé dish and bake for 30-40 minutes, until golden brown. Serve immediately.

GOURDS

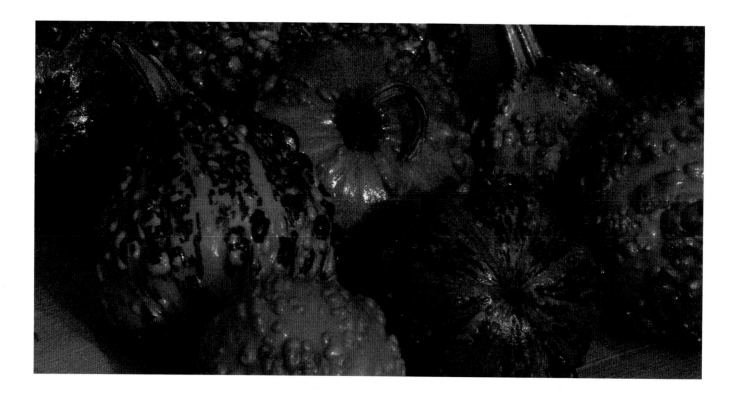

POULTRY AND GAME

Chicken and Paprika Casserole

This is a luxuriously rich, creamy dish, guaranteed to warm chilly autumn bones with its spicy paprika seasoning. Some light vegetables, perhaps stir-fried, steamed or boiled, are all the casserole needs to accompany it.

Serves 4-6
Preparation: 15 mins
Cooking: about 2 hrs

55 g/2 oz butter
1 tbsp olive oil
1 free-range, corn-fed chicken, dressed weight about 900 g-1·8 k/2-4 lb, cut into 8 pieces
115 g/4 oz onions, peeled and sliced
115 g/4 oz celery, trimmed and cut into 2·5 cm/1 in chunks
½ tsp herbes de Provence or mixed dried herbs
2 tsp paprika
1 tbsp flour
450 ml/¾ pt vegetable stock
115 g/4 oz carrots, washed and sliced
115 g/4 oz button mushrooms
450 ml/¾ pt single cream
salt and pepper

Preheat the oven to 190C/375F/gas 5. Melt the butter with the oil in a heavy-bottomed pan over a moderate heat. Lightly brown the pieces of chicken for about 10 minutes and then transfer to an ovenproof casserole, keeping the liquid in the pan.

Place the onions, celery, herbs and paprika in the fat and toss gently over the heat for about 6 minutes until they are just translucent.

Sprinkle with the flour and cook for a further 2 minutes. Gradually add the stock to the pan and bring to the boil. Adjust the seasoning.

Place the carrots on top of the chicken, cover tightly and cook in the oven for 1½ hours.

After about 1 hour of cooking, remove from the oven, add the mushrooms and stir. Re-cover and put back in the oven for the remaining 30 minutes, slightly reducing the heat to 180C/350F/gas 4. Five minutes before the end add the cream and stir.

Serve straight from the casserole accompanied by fresh green vegetables and some boiled potatoes sprinkled with parsley.

Roast Quail

WITH WATERCRESS AND GINGER WINE

Serves 6
Preparation: 10 mins
Cooking: 30 mins

6 whole quail, dressed
2 large bunches of watercress, coarsely chopped
150 ml/¼ pt vegetable stock
30 g/1 oz good quality nut oil
115 g/4 oz butter
55 g/2 oz chopped parsley
55 g/2 oz chopped onion
2 heaped tsp grated zest from an unwaxed lemon
170 g/6 oz fried breadcrumbs (made from a mixture of brown and white bread)
2 tbsp ginger wine
salt and pepper

Preheat the oven to 200C/400F/gas 6 and rinse the cavities of the birds.

Put the watercress in a pan with the stock, bring to the boil and then leave to cool. Once cool, liquidize in a blender.

Mix the butter, parsley, onion and lemon zest into a paste and then spoon this inside the cavities of the birds. Paint the outsides of the birds with the nut oil and sprinkle them with salt and pepper.

Place the birds in a roasting pan and roast for 25 minutes, basting constantly. Remove the pan from the oven and tip up the birds to empty their juices into the pan. Place the birds on a warmed serving dish and surround with the fried breadcrumbs.

Place the roasting pan over a high heat, add the watercress purée and bring to the boil, stirring constantly. Add the ginger wine and adjust the seasoning if necessary. Serve the sauce separately with the birds.

Guinea Fowl

WITH CELERY AND APPLE

You could use dry cider instead of the Calvados in this dish from the Normandy region of France. The result will not be quite the same, however. Ask your butcher for a chicken or game bird carcass to make the stock. Alternatively, you can use 300-450 ml/½-¾ pt ready-made chicken or vegetable stock.

Serves 6-8
Preparation: 40 mins
Cooking: about 1¼ hrs

1 chicken or game bird carcass
2 bay leaves
2 sprigs of parsley
45 g/1½ oz butter
2 fresh guinea fowl, each dressed and cut into 8 pieces
4 tbsp flour
2 onions, peeled and coarsely chopped
3 stalks of white celery, trimmed and coarsely chopped (reserve the leaves for garnish)
3 cooking apples, peeled, cored and coarsely chopped
150 ml/¼ pt dry cider
2 tbsp Calvados
6 tbsp double cream
salt and pepper

Use the carcass to make a stock: put in the pan with the bay leaves, parsley, and a pinch each of salt and pepper. Add just enough water to cover and bring to the boil. Cover and simmer gently for about 20 minutes.

Preheat the oven to 160C/325F/gas 3. Melt the butter in a large deep heavy-bottomed heatproof casserole over a moderate heat. Dust the pieces of guinea fowl with flour then brown them in the butter over a high heat, turning to seal them quickly.

Lower the heat and add the onions and celery. Cook lightly for about 5 minutes, then add the apples. Cook for a further 5 minutes. Remove the casserole from the heat and then sprinkle in just enough of the remaining flour to absorb the fat in the casserole. Cook this flour gently for about 3 minutes.

Gradually add the cider, followed by the Calvados and then 300 ml/½ pt of the strained stock. Bring to the boil slowly and then leave to simmer gently, covered, for about 10 minutes. If the sauce does not cover the pieces of fowl, add a little more strained stock. Season to taste, then place in the oven and bake for about 45 minutes.

Remove from the oven and transfer the pieces of guinea fowl to a warmed serving dish. Put the casserole over a high heat and bring the sauce to the boil. Reduce the heat, add the cream, adjust the seasoning, then pour over the meat. Serve garnished with the celery leaves.

Guinea Fowl with Celery and Apple

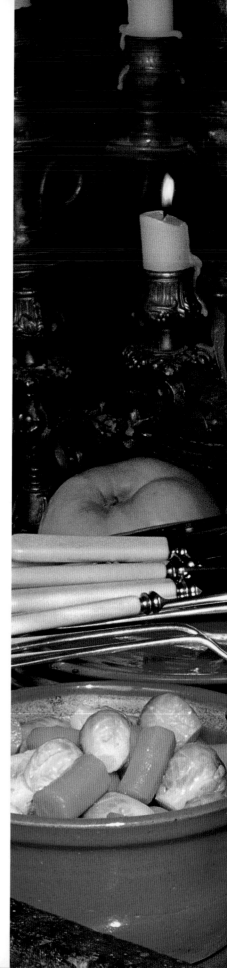

Wild Duck

WITH NECTARINES AND
RED GRAPES

Serves 4
Preparation: 35 mins
Cooking: about 1 hr

2 small mallards, dressed weight about
1·35 k/3 lb each, with giblets

3 tbsp honey

1 tbsp soya sauce

225 g/8 oz red seedless grapes (plus extra
for garnish, if wished)

3 nectarines, sliced (plus 2 extra for
garnish, if wished)

2 heaped tsp grated zest and juice from
1 unwaxed orange

4 tbsp cassis liqueur

85 g/3 oz shelled pistachios

Prick the ducks all over with a carving fork, just below the skin, to let the fat run. Put the ducks, head first, into a large pan of boiling water and boil fast for 20 minutes. Remove from the pan and drain, breast down, until dry.

Preheat the oven to 250C/475F/gas 9.

Place the ducks in a roasting pan and use a pastry brush to coat them liberally with a mixture of the soya sauce and honey.

Put 5 tablespoons of water in the pan and roast in the middle of the oven for 20 minutes, basting every 10 minutes.

Remove from the oven and baste once more. Reduce the oven temperature to 220C/425F/gas 7.

Place the ducks on a wire rack in a clean roasting pan, add 2 tablespoons of water and roast in the middle of the oven for another 20 minutes.

Meanwhile, put the first oven pan over

FARMYARD FOWL
Geese and chickens make their way through
early morning light.

a gentle heat. Add the seedless grapes, nectarine slices, orange zest and the juice. Bring to the boil, add 4 tablespoons of water and the cassis. Simmer gently until the grapes have just softened (add a little more water, if necessary). Pour the sauce into a warmed jug and add the pistachios.

Give the ducks a final five minutes at the hottest the oven will go, then remove the ducks from the oven and transfer to a warmed serving dish.

Serve with the sauce and lots of game chips and a deep green vegetable. Garnish with more grapes and sliced nectarines, if wished.

FRUIT AND CREAM

Great Aunt Sybil's Apple Crunch

This is my great aunt's upside-down apple cake. It is at its best and crunchiest when eaten immediately. Alternatively, you can make the sponge in advance and fill it just before serving.

Serves 6-8
Preparation: 10 mins
Cooking: about 1 hr

200 g/7 oz butter, melted
1 heaped tbsp soft brown sugar
1 generous tbsp golden syrup
550 g/1¼ lb crisp green apples, cored and sliced
juice of ½ a lemon
pinch of salt
1½ tsp baking powder
115 g/4 oz + 1 tbsp caster sugar
350 g/12 oz unbleached plain flour
150 ml/¼ pt evaporated milk
1 egg, beaten
85 g/3 oz cornflakes, crushed
1 large carton (250 ml/8 fl oz) of double cream

Preheat the oven to 180C/350F/gas 4.

Put half the melted butter with the brown sugar and golden syrup in the base of a 20 cm/8 in cake tin. Put 450 g/1 lb of the apples into the mixture and cover the remaining apples with the lemon juice.

In a mixing bowl, combine the salt, baking powder, 115 g/4 oz caster sugar and flour. Add the remaining butter, milk and the egg, beating well until thoroughly combined.

Spread this mixture over the apples in the cake tin and bake for 1 hour. Remove from the oven, loosen round the edges with a knife and turn out on a warm plate. Scrape all the surplus caramel over the apples.

Using another plate, turn the cake upside down, so that the sponge part is now on top again. Leave to cool.

When cool, cut the sponge across horizontally to create 2 layers.

Whip the cream to stiff peaks. Chop and mix in the remaining apples and crushed cornflakes and use this to fill the sandwich. Sprinkle with the remaining caster sugar to serve.

Pear and Stilton Strudel

WITH POPPY SEEDS

Delicate leaves of phyllo pastry, layered with pears and rich Stilton cheese, make this a real special occasion dessert. Any other blue cheese could be substituted for the Stilton.

Serves 6
Preparation: 25 mins
Cooking: 30 mins

450 g/1 lb Conference pears
juice of 1 lemon
grated zest of 1 unwaxed lime
225 g/8 oz Stilton
1 tsp fresh thyme leaves
30 g/1 oz blue poppy seeds
¼ tsp grated nutmeg
8 leaves of strudel or phyllo pastry, 30 x 50 cm/12 x 20 in
115 g/4 oz butter, melted
115 g/4 oz dry brown breadcrumbs
salt and pepper

Preheat the oven to 180C/350F/gas 4 and oil a large oven dish.

Peel, core and cut the pears into 1 cm/½ in cubes. Sprinkle them with the lemon juice and lime zest.

Crumble the Stilton into the pears and add the thyme, poppy seeds (reserving a few for garnish) and nutmeg. Season the mixture to taste.

Place a damp cloth on a flat working surface and place 2 leaves of pastry on it. Brush with melted butter and sprinkle over one-third of the breadcrumbs, followed by one-third of the cheese mixture. Cover with more pastry and continue with these layers until all the ingredients are used up, finishing with a layer of pastry and all layers of pastry being coated with melted butter.

Using the damp cloth, roll up the layered pastry into a large sausage, with the seam on the underside. Transfer to the prepared oven dish, sprinkle with the reserved poppy seeds and bake for 30 minutes. Serve immediately.

COLOUR IN THE ORCHARD (*overleaf*)
Ripening fruits and berries add brilliant splashes of colour amid lush green.

Gooey Meringue

WITH GREENGAGES

If greengages are not available plums can
be substituted.

Serves 6-8
Preparation: 20 mins
Cooking: 1½ hrs, plus cooling

285 g/10 oz caster sugar
5 egg whites
1 level tsp cornflour
1 tsp white wine vinegar
675 g/1½ lb greengages, stoned
150 ml/¼ pt spring water
1 tsp maple syrup

Preheat the oven to 155C/310F/gas 2-3.
Line a baking tray with greaseproof
paper or foil, and oil the lining lightly.

Whisk half the sugar with the egg
whites and beat at maximum speed until
it resembles wet plaster of Paris.

Mix the cornflour with the remaining
sugar and add to the first mixture,
pulsing slowly. Mix in the vinegar.

Spread this mixture on the prepared
baking tray with a spatula and bake for 1
hour. Turn off the oven and leave the
meringue in it for a further 30 minutes.
Remove from the oven. (The meringue
should be hard on the outside, but the
inside will have the consistency of
marshmallow.)

Place the fruit in a pan and add the
water and maple syrup. Bring quickly to
the boil and boil until reduced by half.
Remove from the heat and leave to cool.
When cool, spread on the meringue.

Grape Brûlé

WITH CASSIS

White, red and purple grapes are combined with a luxurious mixture of cream, crème fraîche and thick Greek yoghurt. The texture of the crunchy caramel – made separately and scattered over the top – is a lovely contrast. You could make a large quantity of caramel and keep the surplus in an airtight container for other desserts.

Serves 6
Preparation: 20 mins
Cooking: about 15 mins, 3 hrs ahead

800 g/1¾ lb unrefined white sugar
450 g/1 lb white seedless grapes
450 g/1 lb red seedless grapes
450 g/1 lb purple seedless grapes
6 tbsp cassis liqueur
250 ml/8 fl oz double cream
250 ml/8 fl oz crème fraîche
250 ml/8 fl oz Greek yoghurt

Make a caramel by putting the sugar in 350 ml/12 fl oz of water in a heavy-bottomed pan and bringing it slowly to the boil, making sure that all the sugar has dissolved completely before the liquid actually boils.

Meanwhile line a large baking tray with a sheet of greaseproof paper or metal foil (oil the foil, if using).

Boil the syrup rapidly, uncovered, for about 10 minutes, watching carefully for a colour change towards the end. When it goes from golden to dark brown, remove quickly from the heat and pour into the lined baking tray. (It is possible to make about the size required for your dish when pouring the mixture.) Leave to cool.

When completely set, ease up one corner of the paper or foil. The mixture will start to crack.

Wash, pat dry and halve all the grapes. Mix them well and place flat side down on a large glass dish. Dribble the cassis over them.

Mix the cream, crème fraîche and Greek yoghurt carefully with a fork and then whip until creamy. With a spatula, cover the grapes completely with the mixture. Chill.

When well chilled, place the pieces of cracked caramel over the top to serve.

Notes: do not refrigerate after adding the caramel, or it will sweat. Surplus caramel may be wrapped in greaseproof paper and stored in an airtight container.

Profiteroles

WITH CHOCOLATE AND VIOLET CREAM SAUCE

When arranged in a pyramid with sauce poured over, profiteroles never fail to create an impact. Hand-made violet cream chocolates for the topping of this truly irresistible dessert are available from good department stores and confectioners. You can also experiment with different-flavoured chocolates. Any surplus sauce and topping may be frozen and used to fill and top cakes, etc. You could also use it to add a very special touch to ice cream or fruit.

Makes 36
Preparation: 20 mins
Cooking: 35 mins, plus cooling

115 g/4 oz butter
140 g/5 oz flour, sifted
4 eggs, lightly beaten
pinch of salt

for the filling:
4 egg yolks
115 g/4 oz caster sugar
55 g/2 oz flour
55 g/2 oz cornflour
400 ml/14 fl oz milk
2 tsp essence of violet
one large carton (300 ml/½ pt) double cream

for the topping:
10 hand-made violet cream chocolates
1 packet (100 g/3½ oz) high quality dark chocolate
10 crystallized violets

Preheat the oven to 220C/425F/gas 7 and lightly grease a baking sheet with some butter.

First make the profiteroles: place the butter in a pan with 300 ml/½ pt water and bring it gently to the boil. Continue to boil until all the butter has melted. Add all the flour at once with the salt, beating fast. Continue to beat quickly until the mixture starts to leave the sides of the pan.

Transfer the dough to an electric blender and then gradually add the eggs, one at a time, making sure each is completely incorporated before adding the next. The mixture should then take on a glossy sheen.

Put the mixture in a piping bag fitted with a plain nozzle and pipe 2·5 cm/1 in lengths on the prepared baking tray about 6 mm/¼ in apart. Using a wet finger, smooth the points left by the piping tube.

Bake for about 15 minutes, then reduce the oven temperature to about 180C/350F/gas 4 and cook for a further 10 minutes until the profiteroles are golden brown.

Remove the tray from the oven and puncture each puff with a small sharp-pointed knife to allow the steam to escape. Return the tray to the oven and cook for a further 10 minutes to dry the profiteroles out. Remove from the oven and allow to cool.

While the profiteroles are cooking, make the filling: in a blender combine the egg yolks, half the sugar, the flour, cornflour and 4 tablespoons of the milk.

Put the remaining milk in a saucepan and bring slowly to the boil. Add this to the mixture in the blender, with it running at low-to-medium speed.

Pour this mixture into a saucepan and put over a gentle heat. Bring slowly to the boil again, stirring continuously until the mixture begins to thicken. Remove from the heat, transfer to a bowl and leave to cool slightly. Add the violet essence and leave to sit at room temperature.

Whisk the double cream to soft peaks, then gradually fold in the remaining sugar and beat until incorporated. Fold this into the sauce.

Make the topping: remove and reserve any sugar flower decorations from the hand-made chocolates.

Place these chocolates and the dark chocolates in the top of a double boiler over a gentle heat and allow to melt slowly. If the mixture is too thick to pour, dribble in 2 tablespoons of water a little at a time. Keep warm.

Using a small sharp-pointed knife, pierce the cooled profiteroles near the bottom to create a cavity. Put the sauce into a piping bag and fill the profiteroles with it. Arrange the filled puffs on a serving plate and pour the topping liberally over them. Garnish with the reserved sugar flowers and the crystallized violets. Enjoy!

Grape Brûlé with Cassis ABOVE,
Profiteroles with Chocolate and Violet Cream Sauce BELOW

101

Winter

CHILLY DAYS AND WARM FESTIVITIES

In the countryside, the trees are now stripped naked, except for the evergreens which proudly hold their positions, looking around at the bleak landscape. A few berries blaze in the hedgerow and there are the purple fruits of ivy, the last plant to bear fruit, so late in the season. Rosehips fight the frost and the hawthorn bears its berries boldly, side by side with holly. And there is the magic mistletoe. Norse legend has it that when Freya, the Goddess of Love, cried for her lover, the tears that dropped turned to pearls and a sprig of these pearls was given to her for safekeeping. She hung it between heaven and earth, promising that it would remain harmless as long as it never fell to the ground – hence the tradition of always hanging mistletoe high up.

SPECTRAL SHAPES (*above*)

DUSKY SHADES (*previous page*)

Birds will have a difficult time finding enough food, so suggest that children make a fat cake for the blue tits, sparrows and robins.

Fat Cake

125 g/4 oz cooking fat

75 g/2½ oz stale biscuits, bread and cake crumbs

55 g/2 oz peanuts, sesame and sunflower seeds

Melt the fat and stir in the dry ingredients. Using an old container (margarine tubs suit the purpose well), make a hole in the centre of the container bottom and thread 30 cm/12 in of string through the hole, tying a large knot underneath to secure it. Spoon the mixture into the container around the string and place a heavy plate on top to press it all down very firmly. Refrigerate for 24 hours, before removing the cake from the mould and hanging it in your garden for your birds to enjoy. Put it on a tree close to the kitchen for hours of pleasure from their grateful antics.

December heralds one of the most plentiful times of the year in terms of produce available, as the run-up to Christmas becomes a gallop, and the shops are literally stuffed with provisions of every kind. Cox's apples and tangerines, pork, partridge, venison and plump turkey, goose, duck and guinea fowl, and hoards of local and international fruit and vegetables create exotic and enticing window displays.

Weather permitting, fresh fish should be gracing the marble slabs, and terrines and stews are alternatives to poaching and baking.

Winter is a time for fine food, pleasure and fun. When the weather turns foul, farmers overhaul and repair machinery during the day. If the sun shines they toil ceaselessly against the fast-fading light, whilst in the home preparations of all sorts are being made – cranberry sauce and Christmas pudding, tree decorations and cards, mince pies and brandy snap baskets (see page 125). Many of these things can be made in advance to allow a more relaxing time as the great day looms near.

Start gathering old man's beard, holly, ivy and spruce, pine cones and butcher's broom, to make decorations for the Christmas festivities. Spray fruits and physalis leaves silver and gold to make centrepieces for your table. Stencil paper napkins with your own designs, or just tie pretty ribbon around damask napkins. Refresh pot pourri and surround candles with small pine cones scented with aromatic essential oils. Place them in guests' bedrooms for a pleasant surprise and hang up the orange pomanders which will now be ready (see page 78). Throw pine needles on open fires to compete with the delicious aromas of the kitchen.

Feed the furniture after weeks of central heating and open fires. Mix traditional beeswax polish to revitalize mahogany, oak and pine.

Beeswax Polish

85 g/3 oz beeswax

30 g/1 oz white wax, or ½ standard sized candle

600 ml/1 pt white spirit

600 ml/1 pt hot water

1 tbsp washing up liquid

Over a moderate heat and using an old saucepan, melt the wax. Remove from the heat and slowly stir in the white spirit. Mix the washing up liquid with the water and gently add the wax mixture. Let it cool, stirring occasionally, then put into screw-top jars and label very clearly.

When using, allow the wax some time to sink into the furniture before polishing off with a clean cloth.

Spend a day making home-made chocolates. Most kitchen shops sell the moulds and it is possible to be really creative using endless combinations of your choice. The most important thing is to use only high quality chocolate. Try fresh cream and black cherry, crystallized stem ginger, marshmallow, marzipan, peppermint and fresh fruit, and sultanas soaked in liqueur. Wrapped in plain cellophane paper and tied with a pretty ribbon, they are a great standby for small gifts and a lovely present to receive. As a special treat, let children, under supervision, make toffee apples in the kitchen (see page 108).

After the excitement of the Christmas feasting, marmalade-making and storecupboard food take precedence. Seville oranges and other citrus fruits can be found everywhere. As well as the conventional recipe for the most traditional of breakfast foods, Seville marmalade (see page 24), be bold and mix citrus fruits for exciting new flavours. Roast sunflower and sesame seeds, bake pine kernels with garlic in good oil, toast dulse (see page 21) and other sea vegetables. Store them all in screw-top glass jars to use on salads, to sprinkle on vegetables or simply to enjoy as a nibble. Make blueberry vinegar from berries you have dried in summer.

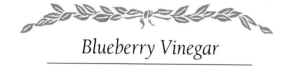

Blueberry Vinegar

115 g/4 oz dried blueberries
white wine vinegar

Place the blueberries in a glass bowl and cover generously with the white wine vinegar, so that it comes at least 10 cm/4 in above the berries.

Cover with muslin and position on a light window sill for 2 weeks.

At the end of this time, strain the vinegar through a cheese cloth. Pour it into a dry sterile jar with a cork or screw top. Pop 3 or 4 blueberries into the jar, seal and label.

Dress up warmly in woollen scarves and coats, fur-lined boots and weatherproof hats to take brisk country walks. Search for animal tracks and birds' feet marks in the mud or under icy puddles, and then, to allow blue noses to regain their natural pink, come home to Winter Warmer tea.

Look out of your window at dusk after a cold but sunny day: as the mist hangs a foot above the warm earth, watch the cows moving silently through it like a mobile domino game, and listen to the screech owl sending its eerie warning to small mammals on the ground.

Winter Warmer

Serves 4-6 cups

15 cardamom pods
15 whole cloves
1 stick of cinnamon, about 5 cm/2 in long,
broken into pieces
1·75 l/3 pt spring water
3 tbsp clear honey (preferably acacia,
lime, etc, blossom)
350 ml/12 fl oz milk
6 tsp black tea (not perfumed)

Place the cardamom, cloves and cinnamon in the water and bring to the boil very gently. Cover and simmer gently for 20 minutes.

Add the honey and then the milk and simmer again for 10 minutes.

Add the tea and allow to simmer for a further 5 minutes. Remove from the heat and leave to infuse for about 3 more minutes.

Strain into warm cups or glasses.

FROSTED LEAVES
Silvery frosts are one of winter's delights.

MENUS *for Winter*

BREAKFAST
Mexican Bollilos with Walnuts and Olive Sauce (p. 115)

LIGHT LUNCH
Baked Marrow with Parsnip, Carrot and Potato (p. 114)

Mixed Nut Croustade (p. 116)

Frosted Grapes (p. 124)

LUNCH
Venison Fondue with Juniper Berries (p. 122)
or
Boiled Bacon with Herb Dumplings (p. 119)
Naughty Potatoes (p. 114)
Baked Onions (p. 114)
Quince, Mulberry and Apple Roll (p. 124)

TEA
Cranberry Bread (p. 111)
Sweetheart Meringues (p. 125)
Toffee-Dipped Fruit and Nuts (p. 118)

LIGHT SUPPER
Phyllo Parcels with Artichoke Hearts and Roquefort (p. 112)
Grouse Breasts with Cranberries (p. 123)
Winter Salad with Warm Vinaigrette (p. 112)
Brandy Snap Baskets with Angelica Cream (p. 125)

DINNER
Bean, Pepper and Potato Soup (p. 112)
Ham en Croûte (p. 119)
or
Pork Medallions with Sloe Gin and Wild and Brown Rice (p. 122)
Broccoli with Roasted Dulse Seaweed (p. 114)
Marie's Wicked Chocolate Mousse (p.124)

PREPARATION

Toffee Apples

You will need wooden skewers or lolly sticks to hold the toffee apples, and coloured plastic wrapping adds to their appeal. After coating with toffee you can roll the apples in chopped nuts if you wish.

Makes 8
Preparation: 10 mins
Cooking: 15 mins, plus cooling

1·1 1/2 pt spring or filtered tap water
900 g/2 lb granulated sugar
70 g/2½ oz liquid glucose
½ tsp natural red food colouring (optional)
8 hard green apples (preferably Granny Smiths)

Put the water in a pan and place over a low heat. Add the sugar and the glucose and stir to dissolve.

Turn the heat to high and bring the syrup to the boil, uncovered. If you have a cooking thermometer, let the syrup boil until the temperature reaches 143C/ 290F. Otherwise, when small bubbles start popping on the surface and the syrup thickens and turns a light golden colour, test for 'doneness': drop a teaspoonful of the syrup into a saucer of cold water – the toffee is ready if it crackles and hardens.

Remove from the heat, stir the food colouring in thoroughly, if using, and place the pan in a larger pan of hot water to prevent the toffee from cooling too quickly. There must be no bubbles left and the syrup must be smooth before

beginning to dip the apples.

Stick a wooden skewer into each of the apples. Tilting the syrup pan slightly, dip the apples into the syrup and turn them to coat evenly all over.

Remove the apple slowly, making sure there are no air bubbles under or in the syrup. (These air bubbles form if the operation is done too quickly!) Repeat until a coating of the required thickness is achieved.

Place the toffee apples on a greased oven dish, putting them down squarely and firmly to form a steady base.

When the toffee is hard, wrap each apple in a square of plastic wrap (coloured, if possible, for an attractive appearance) and tie a tag around the stem, making sure the wrapping is airtight. Chill until required.

These toffee apples are best enjoyed within 24 hours, but will keep for 2 or 3 days.

Ginger Beer

It is little more than a generation ago that many people made their own ginger beer.

There used to be a belief that it would bring bad luck if the 'plant', or starter, was not divided and one half given away each week. Once word gets around that you have such delicious home-made ginger beer, your friends will no doubt want you to revive this custom and supply them with 'plants'. If you decide to give them the finished product instead, it's fun to search out old-fashioned ginger beer bottles to pour it into.

Makes two 9 l/1 gallon jars
Preparation: 10 mins, 1 week ahead

7 tsp sugar
7 tsp ground ginger
juice of 4 lemons
900 g/2 lb sugar
1·1 l/2 pt hot water

for the 'plant':
30 g/1 oz dried yeast
1 tbsp ground ginger
1 tbsp sugar
575 ml/1 pt water at blood temperature

First make the plant: put all the ingredients into a screw-top jar and mix the ingredients well. Put the lid on loosely (do not seal tightly) and stand it in a warm place (but not by a window – 18-30C/65-85F is ideal).

Every day for the next week, add 1 teaspoon each of sugar and ginger. At the end of the week, strain the liquid from the plant carefully through a clean muslin cloth into two 9 l/1 gallon earthenware jars.

To each jar add 2·2 1/4 pt of cold water, half the lemon juice and half the sugar. Top this with 575 ml/1 pt of very hot (but not boiling) water in each jar. Seal tightly with some cork cut to shape and leave for 1 week undisturbed.

Note: the sludge retained after straining may be re-used ad infinitum. Divide it between 2 jars and add 1 teaspoon each of ground ginger and sugar and 575 ml/1 pt of blood-temperature water to each. Proceed as described above.

Stained Glass Window Biscuits

Makes about 18
Preparation: 5 mins, 45 mins ahead
Cooking: about 15 mins

55 g/2 oz icing sugar, sifted
1 tbsp milk
170 g/6 oz flour
115 g/4 oz butter (or equal parts butter and margarine)
½ tsp vanilla essence
115 g/4 oz assorted boiled sweets (including plain coloured, stripey, etc)

Combine the sugar, milk, flour, butter (or butter and margarine) and vanilla and knead the mixture until it is a pliable dough. Cover with plastic film and chill for 45 minutes.

When well chilled, preheat the oven to 200C/400F/gas 6 and roll out the dough on a floured surface. Cut it into decorative shapes, or use pairs of assorted pastry cutters (stars, hearts, trees, gingerbread men, etc) in two sizes to cut out shapes.

Cut a smaller and larger version of each shape and press one on the other so as to leave a border of about 1 cm/½ in all round. Pierce the top with a tiny hole, if intending to use as a tree decoration, or to hang up somewhere.

Place the shapes on a sheet of grease-proof paper or a greased baking tray. In the middle of each shape, either put a single sweet or half each of 2 different sweets with contrasting colours – be creative with the colours!

Bake for 7 minutes at the top of the oven, then 7 minutes in the middle of the oven, or until the sweets have melted. Leave to cool on the baking tray.

These biscuits make a perfect Christmas tree decoration.

Stained Glass Window Biscuits

Cranberry Bread

WITH PECAN NUTS

Makes two 450 g/1 lb loaves
Preparation: 15 mins
Cooking: about 1¼ hrs

200 g/7 oz granulated sugar
200 g/7 oz soft brown sugar
450 g/1 lb unbleached flour
4 tsp baking powder
1 tsp bicarbonate of soda
2 tsp sea salt
115 g/4 oz pecans
115 g/4 oz fine wheatgerm
grated zest from 4 unwaxed oranges
(about 6 tbsp)
450 ml/¾ pt fresh cranberries
2½ tbsp corn oil
250 ml/8 fl oz fresh orange juice
125 ml/4 fl oz warm spring water
2 eggs, lightly beaten

Preheat the oven to 180C/350F/gas 4 and grease two 450 g/1 lb loaf tins.

Combine all the dry ingredients together in the bowl of an electric blender or processor, using the slow pulse.

Add the mixed liquid ingredients, again using the slow pulse for about 3 minutes so as to keep the fruit and nuts as lumps rather than completely liquidizing them.

Spoon the mixture into the prepared loaf tins and bake for about 65 minutes, or until the sides slightly come away from the sides of the tins. Remove from the oven, turn out of the tins and cool on a wire rack.

Cranberry Bread with Pecan Nuts LEFT,
Ginger Beer RIGHT

VEGETABLES

Bean, Pepper and Potato Soup

WITH GARLIC

Serves 6-8
Preparation: 15 mins
Cooking: about 45 mins

45 g / 1½ oz butter
1 tbsp olive oil
3 garlic cloves, peeled and sliced
1 large onion, peeled and sliced
*2 leeks, washed, trimmed and cut into
1 cm / ½ in slices*
*3 sweet peppers (preferably of different
colours), halved, deseeded and chopped*
1·1 l / 2 pt vegetable stock
*450 g / 1 lb potatoes, peeled and cut into
small chunks*
225 g / 8 oz cooked flageolets
1 tsp chilli powder
rock salt

Melt the butter with the oil in a heavy-bottomed pan over a low heat. Add the garlic and cook gently for about 3 minutes, stirring constantly. Then add the onion and the leeks. Cook for a further 5 minutes, then add the peppers and stir-fry for 5 minutes more.

Add the stock, followed by the potatoes, and bring to the boil. Reduce the heat and simmer gently for about 25 minutes. Stir in the chilli powder.

Add the beans and bring back to the boil. Season with salt and serve.

Winter Salad

WITH WARM VINAIGRETTE

There's no need to forget salads just because it's winter. In fact, many substantial winter dishes cry out for refreshing crisp vegetables to accompany them. You could try Blueberry Vinegar (see page 106) on the salad instead of the vinaigrette here.

Serves 4-6
Preparation: 10 mins

*2 bunches of watercress, washed and
trimmed*
2 cooked beetroot, peeled and chopped
2 thin courgettes, grated
*1 bunch of spring onions, cleaned, trimmed
and chopped*
2 tbsp chopped pecans
½ tbsp coarsely chopped parsley
6 tbsp hazelnut oil
2 heaped tsp Dijon mustard
1½ tsp Japanese rice vinegar

Mix the watercress, beetroot, courgettes and spring onions together in a large salad bowl. Sprinkle over the pecans and parsley.

Mix the oil, mustard and vinegar in a small pan and heat very gently until warmed through, then pour over the salad. Serve immediately.

Phyllo Parcels

WITH ARTICHOKE HEARTS
AND ROQUEFORT

Other blue cheeses can be substituted in this recipe but Roquefort has a perfect affinity with the artichokes. The little parcels make ideal pre-dinner nibbles, or you could serve them as a starter. They also freeze well.

Makes about 24
Preparation: 25 mins
Cooking: 45 mins

85 g / 3 oz butter
*8 spring onions, including green stalks,
chopped*
*1 tin (400 g / 14 oz) of artichoke hearts,
drained and chopped small*
2 tbsp flour
200 ml / 7 fl oz milk
115 g / 4 oz Roquefort
225 g / 8 oz phyllo pastry
sunflower oil, for deep-frying
salt and pepper

Melt 30 g / 1 oz of butter in a pan over a moderate heat. Add the spring onions (including the stalks) and cook gently for about 3 minutes. Add the artichokes and allow to heat through.

Increase the heat, add the flour and allow to cook thoroughly. Gradually add the milk to make a smooth sauce. Remove from the heat and allow to cool.

When the mixture is completely cool, add the cheese and combine gently. Season to taste. Melt the remaining butter gently in a small pan.

Spread out the pastry one sheet at a time and paint with melted butter (the pastry dries very quickly, so keep it in the packet until the last minute and cover it with a slightly damp cloth when unwrapped). Cut each sheet into 7·5 cm/ 3 in strips.

Spoon a generous teaspoonful of mixture on to the end of each strip.

Taking a corner of the pastry, fold it over to form a triangle. Fold that triangle up over the remaining pastry and continue this way until the end of the strip is reached. Trim if necessary.

When all the mixture is used up, deep-fry the parcels in the oil, preheated to hot, in batches. Drain the cooked parcels well and pat dry on kitchen paper

Winter Salad with Warm Vinaigrette LEFT, *Phyllo Parcels with Artichoke Hearts and Roquefort* RIGHT

towels. Keep in a warm oven until all are ready. Serve as a starter or with drinks.

Note: be careful when adding salt, as Roquefort is a very salty cheese.

Baked Onions

Serves 6
Preparation: 5 mins
Cooking: 1 hr

6 large onions
6 tsp chopped hazelnuts
6 tsp hazelnut oil
6 tsp soft brown sugar
6 tsp shoyu sauce

Preheat the oven to 200C/400F/ gas 6.

Do not peel the onions, but trim them slightly and level off their bottoms so that they will sit upright in the baking tray. With a sharp knife, make a deep cross halfway down each onion from the top. Gently force the cavity open, making sure the flesh does not break.

Drop a teaspoonful each of nuts, oil, sugar and sauce into the cavity of each onion.

Bake in the oven for 1 hour (adding a tablespoon or two of water to the pan, if necessary).

Broccoli

WITH ROASTED DULSE SEAWEED

The sea vegetable dulse (see page 21) may be unfamiliar to you but it is well worth trying. It is hugely high in mineral content and deliciously crunchy when roasted.

Serves 6-8 as an accompaniment
or 4 as a main course
Preparation: 10 mins
Cooking: about 15 mins

55 g/2 oz dried dulse seaweed
900 g/2 lb broccoli
55 g/2 oz butter
salt and freshly ground black pepper

Preheat the oven to 200C/400F/gas 6.

Put the dulse in a baking dish in the oven for about 10-15 minutes, until crunchy to the touch.

Put the broccoli in a large pan of boiling water and cook for 5 minutes, stirring constantly. Remove from the water while the broccoli is still crunchy, drain well and toss in the butter with salt and pepper to taste.

Place the broccoli in a warmed serving dish, crumble the dulse over the top and serve immediately.

Naughty Potatoes

A stuffing of rich garlic cream cheese explains the 'naughty' in the title of these potatoes. You could quite easily use any other cheese of your choice. however.

Serves 6
Preparation: 15 mins
Cooking: 1½ hrs

6 large baking potatoes
1 packet (142 g/5 oz) garlic Boursin cheese
(or any favourite cheese)
1 tbsp olive oil
1 tbsp rock salt

Preheat the oven to 190C/375F/gas 5.

Scrub the skins of the potatoes clean. Using an apple corer, extract a section from the middle of the potato, going in from both ends if necessary. Reserve the pieces extracted.

Into the cavities, stuff the Boursin cheese, leaving enough room to plug the holes with a short piece of the potato which was removed.

Paint the stuffed and plugged potatoes with the olive oil and then sprinkle them with rock salt. Bake for 1½ hours and serve immediately.

Baked Marrow

WITH PARSNIP, CARROT AND POTATO

This is also very good with grated cheese, especially fresh Parmesan, sprinkled over the top.

Serves 4-6
Preparation: 10 mins
Cooking: 1 hr

6 carrots
6 potatoes
6 parsnips
1 large green vegetable marrow, weighing about 900 g-1·35 k/2-3 lb
1 tsp freshly grated nutmeg
85 g/3 oz butter
salt and pepper

Preheat the oven to 190C/375F/gas 5.

Clean and slice the carrots, potatoes and parsnips. Parboil them for 5-6 minutes. Drain well and then put them to one side.

Slice the marrow lengthwise and remove the seeds. Into the cavity of both halves put the potatoes, carrots and parsnips. Sprinkle with the nutmeg and salt and pepper. Dot with butter, cover with metal foil and bake for 50 minutes.

NUTS

Mexican Bollilos

WITH WALNUTS AND
OLIVE SAUCE

This spindle-shaped bread is eaten in
homes and sold on streets all over
Mexico during the festival of the Day of
the Dead. It is also left as an offering at
the graveside of departed friends and
relatives so that the spirits can take the
bread when they come back to visit at
this time.

Makes 18
Preparation: 20 mins, 3 hrs ahead
Cooking: 25 mins, plus cooling

8 g/¼ oz active dried yeast or
15 g/½ oz fresh yeast
450 ml/¾ pt lukewarm water
30 g/1 oz soft margarine, for greasing
550 g/1¼ lb strong white flour, sifted
2 tbsp unbleached granary flour
1½ tsp fine sea salt
finely ground black pepper

for the sauce:
3 tbsp olive oil
4 onions, peeled and sliced
4 large tomatoes, coarsely chopped
½-1 tsp chilli powder
3 tbsp tapenade (crushed black olives)
3 tbsp crushed young walnuts
salt and pepper

Preheat the oven to 200C/400F/gas 6.
Place the yeast in a small bowl and add
150 ml/¼ pt of the lukewarm water.

Soften and stir the yeast in the water and
leave in a warm place.

Grease a large mixing bowl with the
margarine and add the white and granary
flours. Stir the remaining lukewarm
water along with the salt into the yeast
mixture. Stir thoroughly and then
gradually add to the flour, blending it in
with the hands. When all the water has
been added the dough should leave the
sides of the bowl and be slightly sticky.

Place the dough on a floured surface
and knead until it spreads easily and
becomes smooth and elastic. Put the
dough back into the greased bowl, cover
with a damp cloth and leave at room
temperature for about 2 hours, until
almost doubled in size.

Punch the air out of the dough with
the fists and knead for about 2 minutes.
Leave again, covered, for about 1 more
hour. (This is a slow-rising bread, and
must be allowed its full proofing time!)

Preheat the oven to 200C/400F/gas 6
and grease a baking tray. Remove the
dough from the bowl, knead again for
about 5 minutes, then divide into 2
pieces. Roll each piece into a 46 x
150 cm/18 x 6 in oblong. Roll these into
cylinders and then cut each across into 9
slices. Form a spindle shape from each
piece by pinching one end flat.

Arrange on the baking tray and brush
with water. Sprinkle the pepper on top
and then bake for about 20-25 minutes,
or until golden. Remove and cool on a
wire rack.

Meanwhile, make the sauce: heat the
oil in a heavy-bottomed pan and gently
cook the onions until transparent. Add
the tomatoes and stir until soft. Add
chilli powder to taste and leave to

simmer for 10 minutes. Season to taste
then stir in the tapenade and walnuts.

Serve piping hot as a dip, with the
warm bollilos.

Variations: pine nuts or pecans may be
substituted for the walnuts in the sauce.

Fried Cashews

Serves 6
Preparation: 5 mins
Cooking: 5 mins

450 g/1 lb raw cashews
½ tsp fine sea salt
sunflower oil, for deep-frying
freshly ground black pepper (optional)

Set a 20 cm/8 in deep heavy-bottomed
pan over a moderate heat. Pour in the oil
to a depth of 2·5 cm/1 in.

Allow to heat up until hot, then add
half of the nuts, stirring until they
become golden brown.

Using a slotted spoon, remove them
from the pan, carefully draining off any
excess oil. Place the cooked nuts in a
metal sieve, set over a bowl so that any
drips of oil can be returned to the pan.

Repeat with the remaining nuts.

Place all the cooked nuts on kitchen
paper and sprinkle with the salt and
some pepper, if wished. Serve warm.

Note: the oil, when completely cool,
may be filtered and stored in an airtight
screw-top jar in the refrigerator for re-
use. It enhances the flavour of each
subsequent cashew cooking (but do not
use more than 4 times!).

Mixed Nut Croustade

A croustade is a crunchy crust made from breadcrumbs and, usually, nuts. It is a very useful alternative to a pastry crust and can hold a variety of fillings.

Serves 6
Preparation: 10 mins
Cooking: 30 mins

55 g/2 oz butter, cut into small pieces
115 g/4 oz ground almonds
55 g/2 oz soft brown breadcrumbs
55 g/2 oz soft white breadcrumbs
45 g/1½ oz flaked almonds
45 g/1½ oz pine nuts
45 g/1½ oz hazelnuts
½ tsp herbes de Provence
2 garlic cloves, crushed
freshly grated Parmesan

for the filling:
55 g/2 oz butter
2 onions, peeled and sliced
6 tomatoes, blanched, peeled, deseeded and sliced
225 g/8 oz flat mushrooms, washed and sliced
2 tbsp unbleached granary flour

150 ml/¼ pt milk
150 ml/¼ pt single cream
½ tbsp chopped fresh coriander
½ tsp ground coriander
1 tbsp chopped fresh parsley
salt and pepper

Preheat the oven to 230C/450F/gas 8 and grease a 17·5 cm/7 in ovenproof dish.

Rub together the butter, ground almonds and breadcrumbs. Then add the other nuts, the herbs and the garlic and mix thoroughly.

Line the dish by pressing the mixture firmly into it to a depth of about 1 cm/ ½ in and bake for about 15-20 minutes, or until golden brown.

Meanwhile, make the filling: melt the butter in a pan over a moderate heat and sauté the onions and tomatoes until tender. Add the mushrooms and cook for a further 3 minutes.

Add the flour, stir gently for about 4 minutes, then reduce the heat and gradually stir in the milk and cream mixed together. Cook until the sauce thickens and then add the herbs and coriander and season the sauce to taste.

When the croustade is cooked, increase the oven temperature to 250C/ 475F/gas 9. Spoon the filling into the croustade and bake for a further 5 minutes. Sprinkle over the freshly grated Parmesan just before serving.

Mixed Nut Croustade LEFT, *Fried Cashews* RIGHT (p.115)

Toffee-Dipped Fruit and Nuts

Preparation: 20 mins
Cooking: 20 mins, plus cooling

clementines
baby pineapple, peeled, cored and sliced into rings
Brazil nuts, hazelnuts, macadamia nuts cleaned of any surface pith or shell
Cape gooseberries (physalis)
strawberries, wiped but not hulled
star fruit
seedless grapes

425 g/15 oz granulated sugar
150 ml/¼ pt spring or filtered tap water
chopped crystallized stem ginger (optional)
chopped hazelnuts or almonds (optional)

Skin and segment the clementines, leaving the membrane intact. Remove the hard centres from the pineapple rings and cut them into bite-sized pieces. Pierce each nut and piece of fruit with a cocktail stick and *very* lightly oil a baking tray.

Place the sugar and water in a heavy-bottomed pan over a high heat and stir constantly until all the sugar has dissolved. Do not allow to boil until it has! Boil rapidly, uncovered and without stirring, until the syrup turns a golden brown colour. Watch attentively!

Remove the pan from the heat and test by dropping a teaspoonful of syrup into a bowl of cold water. The toffee should set instantly. If it does not, boil for a few minutes more and do the test again.

When ready, remove from the heat and dip the nuts and fruit in the toffee, one piece at a time. Drain away excess back into the pan. Sprinkle with (or roll in) chopped crystallized ginger or nuts as preferred. Leave to cool on the oiled baking tray. Do not refrigerate as this will make the toffee sweat.

RAINDROPS ON CAMELLIAS
Flower heads create a spectacular, if short-lived, display.

MEAT AND GAME

Ham en Croûte

A Continental alternative to the traditional English baked ham. In Italy this wonderfully festive dish would be served with glacé fruits.

Serves 8-20
Soaking: 3 hrs
Preparation: 2½ hrs, 24 hrs ahead
Cooking: 40 mins

1 ham on the bone, weighing about
2·7 k/6 lb
2 large carrots, peeled and cut into chunks
2 large onions, peeled and quartered
2 stalks of celery
6 whole cloves
2·2 l/4 pt vegetable stock
1 bottle (750 ml/27 fl oz) dry white wine
115 g/4 oz Dijon mustard
675 g/1½ lb puff pastry
1 egg, lightly beaten
45 g/1½ oz butter
45 g/1½ oz flour
salt and pepper

Soak the ham, totally submerged, in cold water for 3 hours.

Empty the pan of water and then add the vegetables, cloves, 1·6 l/3 pt of stock and the wine to the ham.

Bring the liquid to near boiling point then cover. Reduce the heat and simmer for 2 hours. Remove the pan from the heat and leave the ham to cool completely in the stock.

When quite cool, preheat the oven to 220C/425F/gas 7. Drain the ham and cut off any fat from the surface and coat the ham with the Dijon mustard.

On a cool surface, roll out the pastry to the thickness of about 6 mm/¼ in and completely encase the ham in the pastry.

Seal any edges with beaten egg and pinch closed, then glaze the surface of the pastry all over with egg. Decorate with pastry leaves or flowers, as desired, and glaze these.

Cook on a slightly dampened baking tray in the centre of the oven for 40 minutes.

Meanwhile, strain some of the liquid from the vegetables in the pan. Make a sauce by melting the butter in a small pan and then adding the flour, cooking thoroughly and then gradually adding the remaining 575 ml/1 pt of stock. Bring to the boil, simmer for a few minutes and then adjust the seasoning.

Serve the ham in thick slices with the sauce passed separately.

Boiled Bacon

WITH HERB DUMPLINGS

The perfect hearty winter dish.

Serves 6
Preparation: 10 mins, 24 hrs ahead
Cooking: 1 hr

1·8 k/4 lb ham collar
1 large carrot, peeled and chopped
2 stalks of celery, trimmed and chopped
1 large onion, peeled and chopped
2 tbsp cider vinegar
salt and pepper

for the dumplings:
115 g/4 oz self-raising flour
½ tsp salt
55 g/2 oz shredded suet
¾ tbsp dried mixed herbs

Leave the ham to soak in cold water to cover overnight.

Make the dumplings: mix all the ingredients together well in a bowl. Using as little cold water as possible, a few drops at a time and mixing in with a knife, create a stiffish dough.

Using the hands and working as quickly as possible, mould the dough into 12 uniform little balls. Cover and store in the refrigerator until required.

Discard the ham soaking water and replace with fresh cold water to cover the ham completely. Add the vegetables and the cider vinegar then bring gently to the boil.

Reduce the heat to a gentle simmer and cook for 1 hour, ensuring that the meat remains completely beneath the water at all times.

15 minutes before the end of cooking time, pop the dumplings into the water.

At the end of cooking time, remove both the dumplings and the ham from the water. Keep warm on a warmed serving plate. Strain the vegetables and reserve some of the stock for use as a gravy. Season it carefully (as there is still a good deal of salt left in the ham) and serve with boiled potatoes and lots of crunchy green cabbage.

SLOE GIN (above)
This classic country drink is thought to date
back to the eighteenth century, when
gin-drinking was at its peak. Made in the
autumn from deep blue sloes (p. 78), it is
ready for drinking about three months later, or
for using in recipes such as Pork Medallions
with Sloe Gin (overleaf). It is even better if left
to mature for up to a year.

SNOWY DAYS (right)
Chilly weather outdoors makes fireside feasts
seem even more attractive.

Pork Medallions

WITH SLOE GIN

This is a delicious way to use sloe gin bottled in the autumn (see page 78). Wild and Brown Rice with Orange and Herbs is the perfect accompaniment for the pork (see right).

Serves 6
Preparation: 10 mins
Cooking: about 30 mins

55 g/2 oz unsalted butter
2 tbsp olive oil
1·1 k/2½ lb pork tenderloin, trimmed and cut into 1 cm/½ in slices
125 ml/4 fl oz sloe gin
30 g/1 oz soft brown sugar
115 g/4 oz sloes from the gin (or raisins or pitted prunes), quartered
salt and pepper

Heat the butter and oil in a large frying pan or flameproof casserole over a moderate heat. Brown the pork in that in batches, making sure it is sealed on both sides. Keep it warm in a warmed serving dish.

Reserve the pan juices and pour in half the sloe gin. Stir over a moderate heat to scrape up any caramelized sediment.

Stirring constantly, add the sugar and remaining sloe gin and stir until syrupy. Return the meat and its juices to the pan. Add the extra sloes (or raisins or prunes). Season to taste.

Cover and simmer for about 5-10 minutes, until the pork is cooked to taste. Make a ring of the mixed rice (see right) on a warmed serving plate and put the pork in the centre.

Wild and Brown Rice

WITH ORANGE AND HERBS

Serves 6
Preparation: 5 mins
Cooking: 30 mins

200 g/7 oz wild rice, well rinsed
200 g/7 oz long grain brown rice, well rinsed
zest of 2 unwaxed oranges or firm-skinned tangerines
12 fresh sage leaves
sprig of fresh rosemary
½ tbsp butter or olive oil
2 heads of sage leaves, to garnish
salt and pepper

Cook the wild rice in plenty of boiling lightly salted water for 20 minutes. Reduce the heat slightly and add the brown rice (adding extra hot water if necessary) and cook for a further 20 minutes.

Meanwhile, cut the citrus zest into julienne strips, put in a bowl and cover with boiling water. Leave for 5 minutes. Drain well and pat dry.

Placing the sage leaves one on top of the other, cut them into thin strips with scissors. Remove the leaves of rosemary from their stalks and mix with the sage.

Drain the rice thoroughly and rinse under hot running water. Place in a warmed serving dish and gently mix in the herbs and orange zest tossed in the butter or oil. Season to taste and garnish with the heads of sage.

Venison Fondue

WITH JUNIPER BERRIES

Fondues are a very good way of letting everyone get to know each other around the table – and a very easy option for the cook as the guests do most of the cooking themselves! This version has the added special attraction of venison with an unusual juniper berry sauce. Other meat, such as rump steak, could be used instead.

Serves 6
Preparation: 10 mins
Cooking: 10 mins, for the dip

900 g/2 lb tender venison fillet, cut into 3·5 cm/1½ in cubes
450 ml/¾ pt good quality corn oil
150 ml/¼ pt olive oil
3 whole sprigs of thyme
8 fresh or dried juniper berries
salt and pepper

for the dip:
85 g/3 oz butter
85 g/3 oz diced red onion
2 garlic cloves, diced
10 fresh or dried juniper berries
2 tbsp lemon juice

Mix the oils and flavour them with the thyme and whole juniper berries for a few hours.

Put the venison on a pretty plate and season well. Leave for 5 minutes.

Remove the thyme and juniper from the oil and discard. Start heating the oil to 170C/340F and keep at a steady temperature on a table-top burner.

Make the dip: dried juniper berries should first be soaked in hot water until they swell, then cooked in boiling water until tender. Crush the juniper berries then put the butter, onion, garlic and juniper berries in a pan. Cook gently until tender, then add the lemon juice and season to taste. Place in a small warmed dish.

Guests spear the venison chunks with a fondue fork or wooden saté stick, cook it to taste and then dip it into the juniper berry sauce.

Pork Medallions with Sloe Gin, Wild and Brown Rice with Orange and Herbs

Grouse Breasts

WITH FRESH CRANBERRIES

Cranberries complement grouse well.

Serves 4-6
Preparation: 5 mins, 24 hrs ahead
Cooking: 30 mins

115 g/4 oz fresh cranberries
3 tbsp dry sherry
15 g/½ oz caster sugar
85 g/3 oz butter
12 tender young grouse breasts
salt and pepper

Place the cranberries in the sherry and leave to soak overnight. Next day, remove from the sherry (reserving it) and cook the cranberries in a little water with the sugar until tender.

Melt the butter gently in a heavy-bottomed pan, add the breasts and turn up the heat to moderate. Toss the breasts in the butter, covering them completely and browning them on both sides quickly, cooking for no more than about 4 minutes in all.

Transfer to a warmed serving dish, turn up the heat under the pan to high and put in the cranberries. Add the reserved sherry, bring to the boil, season and pour over the breasts to serve.

PUDDINGS AND TREATS

Quince, Mulberry and Apple Roll

Serves 6
Preparation: 30 mins
Cooking: 2 hrs

½ tsp ground allspice
½ tsp cinnamon
½ tsp fine sea salt
225 g/8 oz unbleached self-raising flour
115 g/4 oz shredded suet
55 g/2 oz apples, peeled and cored and cut into small chunks
55 g/2 oz Japonica quince, peeled and cored and cut into small chunks
55 g/2 oz mulberries, gently washed and patted dry
grated zest of 1 unwaxed lemon
grated zest of 1 unwaxed orange
115 g/4 oz soft brown sugar
55 g/2 oz unsulphured currants
4 tbsp golden syrup

Put a very large pan of water on to boil.

Put the spice, cinnamon, salt and flour in a large mixing bowl. Stir in the suet and mix well. Gradually add just enough cold water to make a firm dough.

Place the dough on a cold lightly floured surface and roll it into an oblong shape about 6 mm/¼ in thick.

Arrange the prepared fresh fruit along the dough, leaving a border of about 2·5 cm/1 in uncovered at the sides. Sprinkle the citrus zest over the top, followed by the sugar and currants. Dribble the golden syrup over the top.

Roll the dough up into a sausage (like a Swiss roll) and wrap it in a wet muslin or linen cloth which has been dusted with flour. Tie the roll at either end and gently place a tie around the middle with a long loop at the top to facilitate its removal from the pan. Gently lower the roll into the pan of boiling water and simmer for 2 hours, topping up the water as necessary.

At the end of this time, remove the roll from the water very carefully, unwrap and place it on a warmed serving dish.

Serve with a good traditional English custard. Old-fashioned, rich in calories, yes, but wonderful!

Frosted Grapes

The frosting can be done 2 or 3 hours in advance but the frosted grapes should not be left in the refrigerator or in a damp atmosphere. You will need some cocktail sticks to hold the grapes.

Serves 8
Preparation: 15 mins

115 g/4 oz red seedless grapes
115 g/4 oz black seedless grapes
115 g/4 oz white seedless grapes
350 g/12 oz granulated sugar
6 tbsp spring water
85 g/3 oz caster sugar

Wash and dry the grapes thoroughly.

Place the granulated sugar and the water in a heavy-bottomed pan over a moderate heat and stir until the sugar has completely dissolved.

Turn up the heat and bring to the boil. Boil until the mixture thickens enough to coat the back of a spoon. If you have a cooking thermometer, the temperature should be 143C/290F. Remove from the heat, but place in a bain-marie or on top of a double boiler to keep it warm.

Quickly pierce small bunches of grapes with cocktail sticks and dip into the syrup, then dust with caster sugar over a bowl to catch the surplus.

Marie's Wicked Chocolate Mousse

WITH HONEYCOMB

Serves 4-6
Preparation: 10 mins, 24 hrs ahead

350 g/12 oz high quality plain chocolate
125 ml/4 fl oz still spring water
85 g/3 oz unsalted butter
115 g/4 oz block honeycomb
225 ml/7½ fl oz double cream, lightly whipped
2 tbsp light rum

Melt the chocolate with the water in the top of a double boiler set over a moderate heat. When melted and smooth, remove from the heat and cool slightly.

Add the butter, stirring gently, and crumble in the honeycomb in large chunks. Add the rum and finally the cream. Fold well and pour into a mould and freeze.

Remove from the freezer 2 hours before serving and stand at room temperature.

Serve with almond tuiles and langues-de-chat (see pages 82 and 29).

Brandy Snap Baskets

WITH ANGELICA CREAM

Serves 8
Preparation: 20 mins
Cooking: 5 mins, plus cooling and filling

3 tbsp golden syrup
85 g/3 oz butter
85 g/3 oz brown sugar
85 g/3 oz plain flour
2½ tsp ground ginger

for the angelica cream:
85 g/3 oz chopped candied angelica
(see this page)
1 tbsp corn and barley malt (see page 24)
1 large carton (300 ml/½ pt) double cream,
whipped to soft peaks

Preheat the oven to 190C/375F/gas 5 and lightly grease a baking tray.

Place the golden syrup, butter and sugar in a heavy-bottomed saucepan over a fairly high heat, stirring constantly. The mixture must not boil, but all the butter should melt thoroughly.

Remove the pan from the heat and stir in the mixed flour and ginger.

Drop generous teaspoonful of the mixture on the prepared tray, well spaced as the mixture will spread. Bake for about 5 minutes, until golden brown.

Remove the tray from the oven and allow to cool briefly before lifting the brandy snaps from the tray with a spatula. Have ready small moulds placed upside down (small coffee cups will do) and place the snaps over them to shape them into baskets while still pliable. Leave to cool completely.

Make the filling: add the chopped angelica and the corn and barley malt to the cream and mix well. Place in the baskets to serve.

Sweetheart Meringues

WITH FRUIT FILLING

Makes 8
Preparation: 20 mins
Cooking: 1¼ hrs, plus cooling

4 egg whites
½ tsp cream of tartar
225 g/8 oz caster sugar
55 g/2 oz chopped hazelnuts
30 g/1 oz chopped walnuts
300 ml/½ pt double cream
small carton (150 ml/¼ pt) of crème fraîche (optional)
1 star fruit
2 kiwi fruit
16 black cherries, stoned
16 fresh strawberries
8 whole hazelnuts
8 fresh mint leaves

Preheat the oven to 130C/275F/gas 1.

Draw an 8·5 cm/3½ in heart shape on some baking parchment and cut out 16 of them.

Whisk together the egg whites and cream of tartar until very stiff. Gradually add the sugar, blending or beating continuously between each addition. Fold in the chopped nuts gently with a metal spoon to avoid losing any of the aeration.

Fill a piping bag fitted with a 1 cm/½ in star-shaped nozzle. Pipe a line of the meringue mixture along the outside edge of 8 of the paper hearts. Pipe the mixture all over the others to cover the paper completely.

Bake the meringue shapes for 1 hour, with the solid shapes on the top shelf and the outlines in the middle. Remove from the oven and allow to cool. Once cool, remove the paper.

Meanwhile, make the filling: gently blend the cream with the crème fraîche, if using, and whip to stiff peaks. Spread the cream over the solid bases, place the outlines on top and fill the centres with the fruit – some sliced, some halved, some whole.

Garnish with the hazelnuts and mint leaves to serve.

Candied Angelica

Although packets of candied angelica are everywhere, doing it yourself is much more fun and more rewarding than a trip to the local store. It tastes completely different too.

Preparation: 10 mins, 2 days ahead

Cut some young angelica stalks into uniform lengths and boil in water until tender. Remove from the water and allow to cool slightly. Peel off the outer skins, place the stalks back in the water and simmer until they turn green. Drain and allow to dry. Place the stalks in an earthenware bowl and sprinkle in an equal weight of sugar (making a note of this weight). Leave to stand for 2 days.

At the end of this time, boil the angelica and sugar mixture until it is clear and green again and drain it in a colander.

Pulverize another equal weight of sugar to a powder (or use caster sugar) and strew this over the drained angelica. Place the angelica on plates and let it stand until thoroughly dry.

LEFT TO RIGHT *Sweetheart Meringues with Fruit Filling, Brandy Snap Baskets with Angelica Cream, Toffee Apples (p.108), Toffee-Dipped Fruit and Nuts (p. 118) (overleaf)*

Index